Uncharted Corners of
CONSCIOUSNESS

Uncharted Corners of
CONSCIOUSNESS

A Guidebook for Personal and Spiritual Growth

GERBRIG BERMAN AND SHELLY SISKIND

**in conjunction with our Soul Group
The Teaching Source of Wisdom with which we walk**

iUniverse, Inc.
Bloomington

Uncharted Corners of Consciousness
A Guidebook for Personal and Spiritual Growth

iUniverse books may be ordered through booksellers or by contacting:

iUniverse
1663 Liberty Drive
Bloomington, IN 47403
www.iuniverse.com
1-800-Authors (1-800-288-4677)

ISBN: 978-1-4620-5705-4 (sc)
ISBN: 978-1-4620-5706-1 (hc)
ISBN: 978-1-4620-5707-8 (ebk)

Library of Congress Control Number: 2011918290

Printed in the United States of America

iUniverse rev. date: 06/27/2012

To our parents,
Boukje and Willem Klos,
and Marie and Hy Weisler,
who were always supportive and
taught us not to be afraid of treading new paths.

CONTENTS

Preface

The practicality of spirituality

After forty years of study, contemplation, and learning, we are proud to present this book. Why did this undertaking take so long to be shared? To answer, we must take you back to its inception.

Our lives and the nature of our communities were much different forty years ago than they are today. Topics that were considered spiritual or psychic in nature were raised only with people with whom one felt safe. Holistic modalities and practices such as yoga and meditation were the exception, not the norm. We got together privately to examine the channelled drawings and writings Gerbrig Berman received. This time and place was not right for us to make our explorations public, nor did we feel ready.

We had no idea that there was a purpose behind the information we were reviewing, but the experience triggered curiosity in each of us – compelling us to learn more. We were in awe; how could we have known that these drawings and words were a graphic access point into another dimension? We never could have predicted that both of us would become recipients of such teachings, or that our work with these drawings and the accompanying words would become so prolific as to evolve into a book. We soon realized that these meditative writings were indeed a window to another world – a spiritual training program for both of us.

Just as the community and the world were different forty years ago, we also were not the same individuals as we are today. We were young mothers and were happily ensconced in the early stages of marriage and childrearing years: new homes, diapers, dinners, community involvements, and many other delightful experiences that were a part of that precious time.

We often wondered how we could reconcile that we were being pulled into a realm well outside our day-to-day experiences. We struggled; it was an effort to make and take the time necessary to retreat into a state of inner quietness. This was not what our lives were all about! We had triggered our curiosity, and we persevered.

As we examined the drawings and processed the meditative writings, we realized that we had somehow connected with a spiritual teaching group – one that gave us access to a world beyond our own. The year was 1981, and we had not yet settled into a rhythm of meeting every Thursday. However when we did connect one morning at Shelly's house, we somehow realized what we were reading on those slips of paper was information that was coming to us in a different way. It was like a stream of consciousness, with subject matters that had a sense of universality.

Suddenly we had begun wrestling with a new way of thinking, questioning our very reason for being alive, and seeking to understand our place in a vast universe. How did this feel? Exciting, scary, intimidating, exhilarating – all of the above. It left us with a lot of unanswered questions. We asked, 'With whom are we connected? And what is our reason for making this connection at this time?'

They responded, *We are an ageless source of wisdom. Everything and everyone in the universe has a purpose. Our purpose is to raise the level of consciousness, and you are our partners.* What enabled us to connect was that as we reviewed the writings, we were in a meditative state, which put us into a shared frequency with our team. This was akin to tuning into the right spot on your radio for a particular station. In time we came to identify them as our soul group, our spiritual teaching team, whom we later referred to simply as the team. It was just like meeting any new circle of people, except this was a non-physical one. We developed a deep friendship with the soul group.

The team alluded to is not another dimension but a part of one's self – a combined group of souls who form a wave that affects a personal change, much like the tide washing up on the shoreline, infusing life, change, and drama to one's boundaries. 'We are here, you are there' is but a concept, as is space, time, and essence. What we write about is a partnership – nothing extraordinary, just the power of the ordinary that, when accessed, is a channel more boundless than the Internet.

The team encouraged us to set aside a regular meeting time. Thursday mornings were soon dedicated to our studies, and we treasured our weekly sessions. This work required a firm and fluid commitment and a disciplined, positive state of mind. At the beginning, we questioned the validity of these transmissions. Nevertheless, the benign nature, beauty, and wisdom of the material we received eliminated all doubt. Our confidence in this odd partnership grew.

We began our weekly sessions by entering into a meditative state. The team gave us information in the form of automatic writings and drawings. The language of the writings bore another cadence, archaic lingo or an outdated cliché. Often we went to the dictionary for help in understanding the exact meaning of words because familiar prose was frequently used in unexpected ways.

We began a progressive dialogue and would initiate questions, seeking guidance in our quest for answers: What is the nature of the soul? How does it relate to spirit? Are there such things as karma and reincarnation? We had a thirst to know if a deeper purpose existed to our lives on Earth.

We were instructed to look into our own silence for answers. We learned to be intensely quiet and to go deep inside ourselves in order to be able to hear the answers to our questions.

Sometimes these answers were heard (clair audial), sometimes seen (clair visual), and often felt (clair sensual). We were guided to be our own masters – Self as resource. The team told us that each had the capacity to link to the mysteries of the universe. We had to turn our attention from the outer world into our inner world – a dimension of quiet and timelessness.

We began to document our teachings, concerned that valuable wisdom would be lost. Ultimately we came to realize this information supported us in our chosen careers, underpinning our ordinary endeavours with a deeper meaning and purpose. It infused in each of us an increased sense of compassion and gratitude for everything and everyone around us. Previously we had thought this information was intended only for us or for the people who came for individual consultations. Because of the expansive nature of the information we received, we realized it was important to make it relevant to a divergent audience. We needed to reach everyone, from soccer moms to consciousness-seeking seniors.

Later, as we reviewed the writings, we realized that we had been taught a flowing sequence of teachings, and we recognized that we had been given access to a wisdom that could heal our pains and deepen the meaning of our lives. We knew we were not alone in this world and understood more clearly that a larger purpose existed in our lives on this Earth.

This realization was both exciting and overwhelming. The team urged us to pass their teachings on to the world because there was universal application. They would applaud us for our progress or even chastise us for our inertia. We once encountered cosmic prodding when told that 2,276 souls were waiting on the other side for us to get organized! This number is a direct quote from the team, which came to us in early morning writing. They obviously weren't always pleased with our work ethic!

Today we have a vantage point that only a certain amount of spiritual living and training can bring. Throughout the progression of this book, the polarity of each of us as authors functioned to our mutual and individual advantage. We felt we had a soul-directed partnership with a contract to be fulfilled. We were grateful to have done so.

We took care to present our teachings in as undiluted and authentic a forum as possible. Extra words and explanations have been included strictly as guides.

We have interspersed various writings and strung them together with text to present a fluid form. All original meditative writings appear in italics when they are embedded within our own prose. This will ensure that the writings are easily recognizable by those who seek them.

This spiritual guidebook is a tool to access your own uncharted corners; it is a practical and applicable self-help book for integrated body, mind, spirit, and soul interaction.

It is with great joy that we send this information out into the world.

Self as a resource

Uncharted Corners of Consciousness is a holistic guidebook for both practitioners and seekers alike, to be used for guidance in the search for the self and its deeper meaning – for an understanding of the nature of the soul and for the eventual inclusion of spiritual meaning into our everyday lives.

We have compiled the team's inspirational teachings, meditations, poetry, spontaneous drawings, and philosophical writings. They are meant for reflection and introspection and are presented in their original forms to allow for study and for inclusion into both personal and therapeutic settings.

It is our belief that every being has a soul group, whether we are conscious of its presence or not. Moreover, because we found that connecting with our group enriched and enhanced our lives, we wanted to make this resource available to everyone. Through our own source of wisdom, the team, we learned that the process of unlocking one's individual uncharted corners of consciousness is available to anyone. This guide is a Self as resource tool to help you access your group and establish your own partnership.

Although some of the material will not be considered light reading, we wish to allow you the opportunity of enjoying our messages from beyond in their purest forms. The rhythm and flow of the writings can be used in a meditative, almost trancelike state to create heightened stillness and awareness. Often the language inducing this state is archaic in nature. What we came to appreciate was that 'old' did not mean 'outdated'.

We were being subtly led into uncharted territory. Our mandate was clearing time and space – physical space, emotional space, and spiritual space. Our spiritual teaching team encouraged us to shake hands with our deeper Self while simultaneously living in the present.

Uncharted Corners of Consciousness is a how-to guide for spiritual seekers. Feel free to randomly open the book, select particular topics, seek out the drawings, or read it from cover to cover. Trust your intuition. If your primary interest is meditative writings and poems, they are italicized within appropriate chapters and are easy to find. Meditative drawings for focusing and contemplation are included at the front of each new chapter; other drawings and mandalas are interspersed throughout the material. We enclose the little mandala drawings in the book as examples, knowing very well that they are very individual expressions of a deeper thought. These drawings are symbols that are offered as meditative tools of study, as visuals to help you access your uncharted corners. They are predominantly used as introductions to the chapters and sometimes punctuate the writings. As mentioned in her bio, Gerbrig's first connection with this method of discovery was through a drawing that she then referred to as a doodle.

Chapter one provides a glossary type introduction of frequently used terms. Begin here if you want to ensure that we operate from a platform of shared understanding, or flip back for easy reference when clarification is needed. Should you wish for additional exercises and techniques, they can be found in the later application chapters, towards the back of the book. There is also a full glossary at the back of the book.

How to use this book

Uncharted Corners of Consciousness will constantly invite you to enter into a meditative state, where mind and body are still and free from logical thought. The book will also provide you with the tools to do so. Use it as a roadmap that guides you towards your most expansive self.

As a first instruction, when reading the following four lines, which you will encounter throughout the book, let your examining and questioning self take a rest and instead sit back and feel the words as they wash over you.

> *Body is the vehicle*
> *Mind the driver*
> *Soul the infuser*
> *And Spirit soars unfettered by earthly concerns.*

These simple four lines are the essence of this book. Were you able to read them from a relaxed place? If yes, how did they sound to you? Or did you read them and interpret them with the mind alone? If your answer was yes to the second, they will remain poetic at best, but if you were able to incorporate a relaxed composure and an open attitude, you were likely able to use the words as a mantra, a repetitive sound and meditative tool used for focusing and centering. This could be your introduction into a place of expanded understanding, and the writings along with the drawings will lead you into an inner exploration of your uncharted corners of consciousness. This exciting journey can change your life as you access yourself as a resource. It is a journey that can link you to the unified and unlimited knowledge of the universe.

Uncharted Corners of Consciousness is a guide for spiritual seekers. You will find that as you proceed through the book, each chapter will address the specific aspects presented in this poem: body, mind, spirit, and soul; what they are; how they work; and why it can be life changing to understand their interaction. In addition to the drawings and writings, we will provide you with a series of exercises and explanations. Though these tools may seem to sometimes be repetitive, repetition and practice will lead you step by step, deeper and deeper into your uncharted corners.

A special note: throughout the book, the transpersonal Self is distinguishable in the writings as starting with a capital letter, whereas the personal or personality self is lowercased.

"Whisperings from the Soul" is included as a supplement to the main book; it is a compilation of mini musings and reflections.

Acknowledgements

We wish to thank our soul group (spiritual teaching team) for their wisdom, guidance, patience, and keen sense of humour.

We also acknowledge and thank our physical group: our husbands, Harvey Berman and Bob Siskind, and our families, who instilled in us the confidence to proceed and who kept us in touch with our immediate reality. Thank you as well to our editor, Karen Graham; our proofreaders; and our clients.

Special thanks to Jo-Anne Berman, Thera Bikkers, Doreen Jensen, Penn Kemp, Andrew Lindsay, and Kim Soltero for their invaluable help.

All of you pushed us to get this into circulation through your infinite patience and ultimate prodding. We thank you for your encouragement and enthusiasm.

Are you awake?
Are you asleep?
Are you out there
or in here,
trying to listen
to voices that have the answers?
Out there or here,
wherever you are,
your silent voice
is right here inside.
You and only you know
what is right.

List of poems

Chapter 16
Artful
Burdened
Haute Couture

Many of these poems are excerpts from *Fragments and Findings,* Shelly's collection of poems and aphorisms; others are from Gerbrig's *Shaman Behind the Mask,* a traveller's narrative. Some come directly from the team and were embedded in the writings, and still others we included as contributions from our editors.

Chapter 1
Identifying the Main Players

Body-Mind-Spirit-Soul

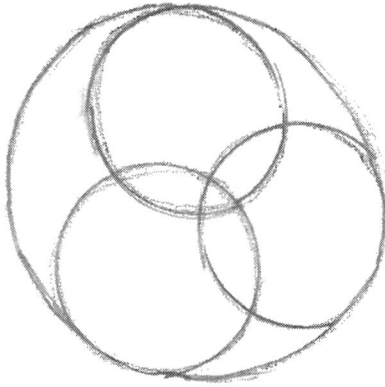

Perhaps we were more receptive to meeting our spiritual teaching team and working with our expanded dimensions, because although our lives were seemingly rooted in a very physical and conventional existence when the two of us connected, experiences with the more universal dimensions were not unknown to us.

As a preschooler I had infused all of my thirteen dolls with whom I slept with qualities, and as a teenager I knew that a Native American man sat beside me as I escaped the bothersome aspects of my life and watched the North Saskatchewan River flow. I always felt safe and protected in his presence. It was not until I met my close native friends and teachers that I learned I was seeing and walking with spirit guides. As a very young child, Gerbrig always felt protected, experiencing that protection as a shield. Later on in the Japanese prisoner of war camp, she clearly remembers her grandfather, who passed away before she was born, coming from the spirit realm with a group of people whom she did not know to check on her and reassure her that she was fine. Though the events differed, the feelings of comfort were imbedded within both of us. For many years we kept these thoughts and experiences private. However, as the years progressed, we realized we were not alone, and because these thoughts had not been encouraged or prodded, they were obviously expressions sprung out of a deeper conscious thought that sustained us throughout our lives with feelings of comfort and trust. It was a relief to meet one another, begin to share these experiences, and discover that there were many others who had similar experiences and feelings. In retrospect, we realize these early experiences made us all the more receptive to the teachings we received in our thirties.

Throughout our study, we encountered the terms soul, spirit, self, and higher Self, and in grappling to understand the difference between them, we asked the team for clarification. Pulling us back to centre, they explained that what is often referred to as peeling the layers of an onion in this sequence of lessons was more like a series of thin slices of the self, scrutinized and decoded. We knew we were in for some heavy learning but did not know what form it would take. We would soon learn that the team first defined the terms as you will encounter them in this chapter and then showed us their various functions and iterations.

In addition to the self-evident physical level, this book explores our non-physical dimension. Whereas the physical level, with its key driver being the body, has eyes, hands, heart, and ears as its central components, the non-physical level has mind, soul, and spirit as its essential players. These writings describe the key elements and examine their importance and interrelationship.

There is a 'vibrational lever' within our body that is the gauge that harmonizes and bridges these events. It listens and adjusts to our external circumstances, striving to maintain balance. The mind, our interpretative mechanism, has the ability to use this regulating power to sift through the information enforced upon us willy-nilly, in a way that is neither enhancing nor depleting. In such instances, keen clarity is self-empowering.

Body is the vehicle,
Mind the driver,
Soul the infuser.
Each has its specific function.

This chapter is a compilation of information that we received over many years of study, long before we knew we would be writing a book. Once we began the process of assembling the information into book form, we realized that the key players with whom you would be dealing needed to be defined.

Body is the physical container. Body is the part of us that takes action.

Mind is calculative and issue oriented. Mind is the part of us that thinks.

Soul is the essential higher thought. Its thought process descends to where deeper love and caring dwell, to the place of feeling, the source of commitment and responsibility. Soul is the aspect that moves us towards selfless service.

Mind is the changing vibrational lever that facilitates change when lessons are learned. Mind helps us to interpret what we have learned on a soul level.

Soul is the reminiscing and transitory aspect of our essence, which is unaffected by outer influences, so that the path of the soul remains the same throughout our many existences. What is affected is the form this expression will take in our present existence. Soul reviews and changes but is unaffected by daily events; it is eternal.

Note: spirit and soul are used interchangeably by some – not so in our writings.

Spirit soars, unfettered by earthly concerns. Spirit is a guiding principle of conscious life, animating body and mediating between body and soul. Spirit guides us in our highest purposes, enlivens the body, and is our go-between body and soul.

The Soul, in its reminiscing and transitory role, is able to glimpse a larger picture: past, present, and future. Soul manifests in us as a thought centre. In accepting the manifesting function of soul, we realize that the physical part, the very creation of man, is a 'thought manifest'. We can be seen as being embodied in a physical vehicle, the body, over which we have taken the reins. Body as well as mind has a vibrational lever that shifts as we adapt to present-day living conditions. Soul can draw on past, present, and future, and when integrated with body, it can actually make our thoughts become reality.

Self is an aspect of soul still influenced by that which surrounds its physical form. Self is the part of us that is connected to and can be distracted by day-to-day events.

Soul is the part of us that first houses the sparkling realization that there is more to us than our mere physical container – a giant step on the path of spiritual awareness. Soul is the part of us that opens us to that place of unconditional acceptance.

People have long sought to pinpoint the essence of their existence. This search often leads into a curiosity about the nature of the soul. Once on the path of spiritual search and unfoldment, there emerges an exquisite dance towards enhancing our relationship with our deeper or higher Self. Once one begins to question why we are here on earth, questioning the soul and if it exists beyond death, they have begun to delve into their uncharted corners.

Interaction: body-mind-soul

We ourselves are a composite of body, mind, and soul – three units melded into one, each functioning according to its own principles. Man or woman in its body governs its existence in a world of demands and privileges, functioning through a deliberate mind and guided by its deeper conscience. Heady stuff!

Heady stuff? Yes, we did find much of the material heady stuff, and yet on the other hand it was pushing us to step outside our comfortable, well-defined spaces. Was our spiritual teaching team trying to lighten things up? And in doing this, were they inviting us to leave our outer projections and enter our interior worlds? We think so.

Interaction: body-mind-spirit

Body and Mind are considered the two vehicles of the human being.

Both have their purposes. Both propel us into the realm of our functioning. Both need appropriate care for their own functioning, and they function according to the care and welfare allotted to them.

Their abilities still depend on a third mechanism within us: the cog in the wheel, the other essence that makes the total within a functional triad. Its entrance into our life is seen just as a cry when lungs are filled with air for the first time. Its exit is merely noticed as a last breath that did not come back to become repeated.

Something came and something left, and in between we were alive, something that made us a loving person able to function, able to make

4

decisions. The equipment in our physical bodies and the circuits of our mind intact and, in perfect working condition, cannot function when this capacity of drawing breath is not there.

In the East Indian mystical tradition, this drawing of breath is called prana, or life force; we call it spirit.

Spirit is an intangible part of us; its essence is described and sought after by theologians and philosophers alike. Known to anybody is the capacity of the body, which the mind has taken leave of, still existing for many years. And we know of the brilliant mind that finds itself within a body that does not allow it any capacity to function. We also know that something did not allow the continuation of that life. Somewhere was one more strength to contend with, one more decisive factor in our being alive or not, one part of ourselves that defies description and that does not function according to our usual descriptive values. A paraplegic would be a perfect example of this: an active mind housed in a paralyzed body. Such a disability did not allow that life to continue in its same form.

The nature of the spirit

Though thought to be elusive, it is, in fact, ever-present: the I or I am, which constitutes the essential part of your being. When you walk, it walks with you. When you speak, it whispers softly from the regions of your heart, for it is indeed heartfelt. When you recognize its presence, then you begin to walk hand-in-hand with a deliberateness of step and direction. For when your spirit is allowed to shine, then too shall you shine; to speak of it as separate is to misunderstand because there is no division, no separation, no duality.

Spirit is your spirit.
Spirit is.
Spirit is you, and you are spirit.

This short poem reinforces the non-separation of an individual from their spirit, as in the expression 'a spirited person'. It came as part of a writing reinforcing the teachings in this chapter on the nature of spirit.

Chapter 2
Tuning in and turning on

Meeting yourself on another level

As we shift from a discussion of the four key elements – body, mind, soul, and spirit – and move into the realm of personal choice, we ask the following question: Does an awareness of soul and its presence make a difference in our lives? The answer is a resounding yes. In our continuing work with this material week after week, we found ourselves asking such questions. And while searching for clarification and understanding, we most often asked the team out loud, presenting our own thought line, and the explanation would come in the form of a written response, though we simultaneously either felt or heard the words. In many cases the team would be aware of us discussing a topic and provide an answer as we talked. This forced us to stop and write something down; invariably, they shifted our way of thinking. The why was given to us in a multitude of ways over many years – the drawings, the writings, the situations with which we grappled, and the results we experienced in therapeutic situations. The breadth of references drawn upon by the team in teaching us held us in awe. Many of the explanations and concepts that our team introduced over the years were very eclectic, drawing from many traditions. They explained:

Uncharted corners extract ancient concepts from Eastern and Western mysticism and integrate them with modern Western life: an updated approach to an age-old adat.[1]

Throughout those years of work, we were reminded that we do indeed live on different levels of existence, and how we deal with things is subjective. Our interpretation depends on the level we access. Such a realization catapults us into accepting responsibility for what we create. It transformed how we handled our daily accomplishments or disappointments. Life took on an element of choice – where we could and did have a direct impact on all aspects of our lives. Nahrajana, the yogi with whom Gerbrig studied in the eighties, said, 'According to Buddha: in any given moment we have seven different choices or courses of action'. The writings tell us that clear thought does not make a clean bill of health or trouble-free days. Rather, we accept that we are dealt a certain hand and are surrounded by certain circumstances of living. We have the ability to better understand the path of the soul. In so doing, we use our circumstances to align with this path. Life is never easy, but to operate on this level or dimension gives a perspective from which we can appreciate and grapple with life's dynamic nature.

All you can be

Seeing ourselves as part of creative spirit and a member of a larger soul essence makes of us, in this existence, more compassionate and understanding humans. Nourishing the body, nourishing the mind, and treasuring the Self on the soul level frees us from any action that favours functioning in a one-sided mode. Working towards integration of these different aspects of the

---

[1]   Adat is an Indonesian or Javanese word referring to the traditional law native to that country.

self as a functioning trinity opens a channel for self-actualization, enriching our total potential.

Once you begin to expand into the fullness of Self, you begin to realize your interconnectedness with your surroundings and all other beings. A feeling of separateness, or seeing anyone else as 'other', dissolves; this expansiveness and inclusivity is enriching.

Thought manifest

Life can be seen as the momentary acceptance of a situation, which is triggered by the soul – a thought manifest. Thought is the reason behind any result. Thought has the potential to create in physical form.

In life, with its many gifts and abilities, there are also many restrictions and constraints. We all will eventually create a unique picture that expresses the choices we have made.

Having established a deeper relationship with our higher Self, or soul self (also referred to as the transpersonal self, the aspect of us that is freed from the constraints of the ego and feels a connection to all that is,) infuses the simplest of actions with unselfish, loving undertones. This gives the smallest task an underpinning of deliberation, referred to as the Zen of doing things.

It triggers us to view our lives and live with a different focus. Needless wants, unfulfilling in many ways, will give way to unselfish giving and sharing. An appreciation of efforts of acquisition becomes an issue of self-realization. Operating on this footing of deliberateness can only serve to support the fluidity of self and enhance our joy in living life to the fullest.

The writings direct us subtly back to the interaction of body-mind-spirit-soul in all our endeavours. The Zen of doing things is designed to wake us up to the notion that the deliberateness of the Zen way should infuse our every action. It is accepting situations as they appear and dealing with them in a straightforward manner. If you have a dog, you will need to walk him, feed him, and care for him. The Zen approach applies a single focus and clarity about our self and our intentions, taking the good with the bad with no judgement attached. The writings also put full responsibility for what we create back into our hands. They do not suggest that we are responsible for the actual creation of the situations, but how we interpret them is unquestionably our choice. We should remind ourselves that thought forms have repercussions: the Zen of doing things follows us into everyday life.

The more we worked with the writings, the more we realized we had to do the work on ourselves before we could comfortably share it with anybody else. There were times when this required us to dodge the bullets of everyday life that were flying at us. Daunting? Sometimes, but for the most part not really; it somehow felt like this obligation was really a privilege. We did use our gearing in sessions prior to our work on the writings to clear up any unfinished items of daily business. Then after grappling with the information given to us in the writings, we would approach our challenges differently, applying the more expansive and inclusive ways of thinking to our individual situations. Little did we know that what we were doing was assembling a toolkit. We brashly wound up applying what we had learned in our work situations. It was like a functioning lab, where we were simultaneously teaching and learning. In looking back we realize that as the information assimilated within us, people would come forward requesting work, and that work took many forms. Gerbrig, who spoke little Spanish, found herself providing nursing care and lecturing on preventative health in a Guatemalan village. In my clinic I encountered seriously troubled clients such as anorexics and cutters, who were referred by doctors or other clients. They seemed open to dealing with their issues in an alternative manner. For both of us, directives on how to work with these people came from the place of self-sourcing and insight that we were being taught.

Our Psychic Blueprint

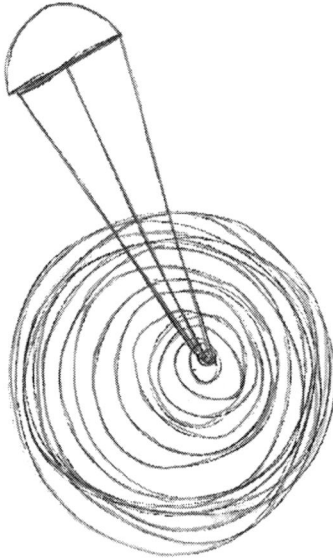

This writing deals with the psychic imprinting based on previous experience that we bring into adult life. This imprinted material must be brought to consciousness and dealt with, or it will unknowingly influence present life situations. Particular conditions that exist in the psyche or mind of a person, our 'personal corporate culture', are self-definitions that have an impact on our behaviour: 'I'm a father', 'I'm a provider', 'I'm a community leader', or 'I'm a failure'. At any given time, we must recognize that we live in specific environments with specific problems, and we must learn to deal with them. Interpretation plays a significant role in determining our ability to cope.

The writings that follow move us into the realm of the transpersonal, the domain of spirit and soul. They speak of moments when we can reach illumination or ecstasy by leaving ego-based behaviours behind, entering into our 'uncharted corners of consciousness'.

Self-knowledge

Self-knowledge and callous scrutinization allow us to overcome and alter a dysfunctional pattern, provided we are aware of the socio-cultural make-up of our psyche.

The degree of stress one experiences is often determined by the response one has towards what is outside oneself and how the mind interprets these events. Treatment of stress should incorporate an understanding of the important role interpretation plays.

Recognition and evaluation of the stress syndrome operating in any situation can allow for a redirecting and rechannelling of responses, which are otherwise harmful and unproductive. Only through such recognition can we work out a new response pattern. A person who is able to evaluate his or her emotional responses to the outside world can start to rechannel his or her own emotional responses. This is more easily achieved when we are functioning within a world with which we feel compatible.

Functioning with our physical and emotional aspects in top capacity is a challenge. Achieving this will result in a feeling of excitement about life and living, responding as a well person, functioning to the fullest. Our emotions and demeanour register themselves in a concrete manner. They express on our face or in our stance as joy or sorrow. What we think has vast implications.

When we are given choice, how do we choose to cloak ourselves?

Interpersonal behaviours

Interpersonal behaviours based on cultural conditioning and learned behaviours enable us to fit into our society and benefit from the results. Altruism and hedonism are the extended feelings given to us to share with our surrounding fellows. As a tool, they are meant to bring changes in our relationships, which can benefit ourselves and others. They are mutually satisfying responses to an ego-based need.

Having this ability to share our mind concept with a high degree of social acceptance brings this special, mind-driven dimension to humankind. It is the extension of this highly developed concept of social interaction into our social and cultural conditioning that makes us adept at coping with our surroundings.

Sightless

Until I perceive, I cannot see.
Until I see, I cannot love as I would.

Transpersonal behaviours

This writing deals with spirit or soul and how their capacities and capabilities differ from our mind – and ego-based interactions. It highlights the spiritual aspects of ourselves to such an extent that it relegates our physical self to a role of minor importance. It even suggests that a withdrawal from the physical can defy the laws of nature, and it touches on the practice of observing the body from afar. Further on it recommends caution while moving into these realms of expanded consciousness, because though much information is held in the unconscious, retrieval of information from this level can be spontaneous and unexpected. Later it explains that with practice we can develop the ability to have immediate recall and to move comfortably from the conscious to the unconscious and back. In this way we develop a valuable personal toolkit. As we add the mind and its abilities to work with these deeper levels, the writing tells us we can influence our well-being. When this connection of spirit to body and mind is well established, body and mind will be channelled into an alignment with our spiritual purpose.

Spirit and soul deal with the nomenclature for the capacity, which springs from within. Mind and interaction are capacities that are basically ego-based. Soul is universal-based: it brings a depth of caring, understanding, and love that does not turn its back to people with their physical challenges; it sees the physical as only a small part of the total. The ability of people to watch themselves from out of the confines of the physical is referred to in Hinduism as illumination. In this state of total ecstasy, we are centred within the point that created us, connected to the All. This is the very core of our being, the breath that blew life into the body, the spark that is neither male nor female. It is a place that just is.

Within a state like this, the physical is hardly a place where the spirit rests. Withdrawal from the physical can result in conditions defying the laws of nature. From conscious memory, our mind progresses to the unconscious: the forgotten memory to the superconscious, our integral intrinsic being.

Through expanded consciousness, our mind can go from the conscious into part of the unconsciousness. Altered conscious states are the means of treading cautiously into this mysterious area. Although we use a great deal of the information stored in the unconscious, we retrieve it mainly in times of automatic and reflex responses. By increasing our awareness, we develop the ability to have a larger concept of the immediate recall with, as benefit, a larger range of responses. The building up of sensitivity to being able to bring forth the response pattern within ourselves is a great tool.

The storage of information on the deeper level is a response to stimuli, which is recorded on the subconscious level. Through flexibility within our own thought process, the mind can be used within a functioning capacity to activate us into our well-being.

Working with an awareness of the width and limits of application of the body, we see the body as being a thought manifest of the spirit, a tool of the mind. Both of them are channelled into a purpose of which the spirit, our link to the universe, is the driver.

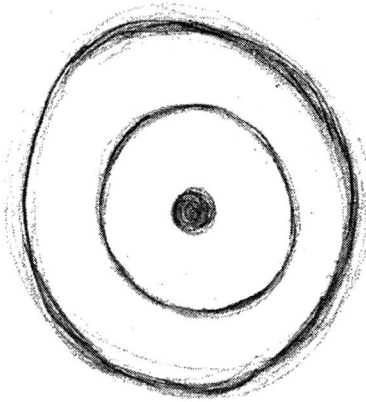

Wholeness: body-mind-soul

Contained within the richness of the following writing is the reminder of both the elusiveness and accessibility of our connection to our deeper aspects. It reminds us of our responsibilities as teachers for the coming generations and places the responsibility for self-awareness and growth squarely in our own laps. It forces us to be our own task masters, assuring

13

us that in the process of being curious and exploring, we extend outward into our surroundings, honing ourselves into fuller human beings. This meditative writing encourages us to not let the din and excitement of modern life obliterate the whisperings of the soul.

We are encouraged to look at the purposefulness of our behaviour, to examine the invaluable role meditation plays in leaving ego-based behaviours behind. This, in turn, can move us into the realms of illumination and ecstasy – worthwhile rewards. These two fragments present different representations of the above information in poetic form; they are offered for your reflection. The subject of meditation, being the tool for accessing these deeper dimensions, is vast and varied.

Every time we sat down to do our work, we had to deliberately curb our busy thoughts and allow our neurons to take on a different way of functioning. We dropped the chatter of our 'must dos' and replaced it with an inner quiet. But first we inadvertently established what might seem an unusual ritual. After greeting one another, we made a cup of coffee and caught one another up on the events of our daily lives. Only then, through a refocusing of our thoughts, could we attune ourselves to the empty, open space of mindfulness, from which we could hear and absorb the lessons. Having done the relaxation exercise given below over and over again, its effects had been permanently lodged in our muscle memory, and movement into the quiet became easy. Eventually all we had to do was sit down, take a breath, greet and thank the team, and begin our work. Our completion ritual was equally peculiar. After our studies we found ourselves famished and would plunk any leftovers onto the counter and munch. The rule was no fuss and fanfare. This scarfing of food was our attuning out; it was a perfect segue back to our daily activities.

Three components, three actions: physical-mental-spiritual, one being a natural continuation of the other function, enhancing and enriching its dimension. A physical without mental interaction, without the dimension of control, has lost its purposefulness and its meaning. A movement that is non-mind directed, without the restriction of a controlled interaction, loses its usefulness and coordination. The mind follows this comparison in a parallel direction. A mental capacity without its spiritual values underlying its thoughts loses the beauty and depth of its function. Thoughts devoid of any deeper spirituality have only the level of reasoning capacity on a mechanical level.

The ability to reason differs from intuition, which is the ability to sense or to feel actions. Intuition has an outcome based on an extension of feelings. A combination of both reason and feelings takes us into a different realm.

In our busy lives, with their heavy interaction with technology and emphasis on left-brain capacity, the exposure to our silent Self is so easily drowned out from everyday life. The discipline of meditation, prayer, and retreat to silence are ways to encounter this dimension within the self.

Re-education and reteaching has to be developed in order to re-establish this relationship. A child daily exposed to the sensitivity of a mind-choosing and to the interaction with the silent Self will have the advantage of easing into adulthood.

Morals, teachings, and friendliness with the interaction of body, mind, and soul are essences not usually included in our descriptions of ourselves. Ask someone to describe himself or herself. 'I am tall, like to read, and love to help people'. 'I am old, a bookkeeper, and sentimental'. We should be able to find within each self-exploration a concept of the trinity within which we see ourselves – physical, emotional, and mental components – and a deeper intrinsic value we hold, a value that is usually independent of the other yet makes itself felt. This intrinsic value is inherent in each of us. Feelings, conscience, and the sense of Self on its deepest level are the essences that the mind feels ready to translate into interactions with our surroundings.

I believe strongly that to be self-governed
is to be liberated, and that harmful aspects are mind-made.
– Dr. Nelson, a member of our spiritual teaching team

Accessing the higher vibrations: giving thanks – place, time, and setting

In order to safely access the deeper Self, this writing encourages us to give reverence by being respectful: say please and thank you and approach your practice or study time from a place of grace. What is demanded is a level of unconditional appreciation, and this unconditional appreciation sets the tone for every moment of our work on this material. The writing states you should offer an invocation, your own kind of blessing, and take responsibility for being the one in charge. There is practicality in this kind of approach, and following the steps works.

Placing the self into a different reference frame is a primary requirement for accessing the deeper Self in a protective way. This can be achieved using many methods, approaches, shapes, and foci.

By saying our pleases and thank-yous, we bring this deeper dimension into our everyday life, moving the mystical into the mundane. We administer and give respect to life, and life forms around us. This elevates ourselves through recognition that we are in a state of grace. It gives us the dignity to acknowledge that we have been able to both give and receive.

Being quiet, setting time, acknowledging silence, sitting in circle, respecting the other, and giving thanks in invocation are means for giving respect and dignity to any form. These actions elevate us to a level where we ourselves are master. It is the love we are and of which we partake. It is the level of unconditional appreciation, the silent smile, which, having fulfilled a higher affirmation of this feeling, is universal in its acceptance.

There is much music around us, many channels to which we tune. It is essential to select the right channel, the place of positivity and inner quiet. Different music calls forward different states of mind and body. The rhythmic beat of music has a strong effect on the body. We cannot expect loud or energetic music to lead us to the soul dimension. Soothing music will help us to withdraw into a state of quiet, where we can reach the domain of the soul. Music can help us attune ourselves to the finer, more positive vibrations. But music is only one tool available to help us reach this place of stillness – clarity of mind and comfort and stillness of body are also essential elements. Taking the following steps will ensure that we are tuned in to the positive and beneficial.

Exercise: a progressive relaxation for use in preparation for meditation

Note: Someone should read the following piece as you do the exercise; alternatively, transpose it to a tape. Ensure your pace is slow and that the voice is calm. Do not rush this exercise; take five to eight minutes to complete it.

Seat yourself in a comfortable position: arms and legs uncrossed, spine straight. Begin by closing your eyes and taking one or two deep breaths in and out. Pause a moment and instruct yourself that you will be assuming a position of alert relaxation. Proceed by focusing your attention on the sound of your breathing, in and out. Do this several times. Then, keeping your eyes shut, allow your attention to shift its focus to a space from five or six inches above your head to the tip of your chin. Imagine you are picking up feelings of tension or busyness, lead them down through your body, and let them drop away into the ground.

When you are ready, shift your attention to your shoulders and down to the mid-back, right through to the front of your chest. Imagine you are picking up feelings of tension or busyness, lead them down through your body, and let them drop away into the ground.

Next, shift your attention to the lower back, through to the stomach. Imagine you are picking up feelings of tension or busyness, lead them down through your body, and let them drop away into the ground.

Move your attention to the upper arm, down through the elbows, and down through to the fingertips. Imagine you are picking up feelings of tension or busyness, lead them down through your body, and let them drop away into the ground. Shift your attention to the legs and the thighs, down through your knees, your calves, and into your feet. Imagine you are picking up feelings of tension or busyness, lead them down through your body, and let them drop away into the ground.

Notice all thoughts, good or bad. Imagine you are picking them up, leading them down, and letting them drop away into the ground. Notice any feelings, good or bad. Pick them up, lead them down, and let them drop away. You should be left with a feeling of relaxation and spaciousness in the body, in the mind, and in the emotions. Take a moment to scan your body and repeat the process if there are any spots left that still need attention.

Quiet the mind and body;
feel a connectedness to all that surrounds;
align to the Higher Self;
be very specific when addressing one's questions or needs;
assume an attitude of gratitude and thankfulness.

Such attention and focus will enable us to retreat into a place of sanctity and protection, ready to connect with the self on a soul level.

When seeking help from the higher dimensions, specificity is critical, or what arrives may not be quite what you bargained for. The following true story happened to a dear friend of ours.

Finding herself in a place of confusion, where things in her life were not going well, Elizabeth awoke at 5:30 one spring morning and went down to the river. From a place of exasperation she said, 'Please, I need clarity'. As she stood on the riverbank, she felt a presence behind her. Curious, she turned around and saw a woman dressed in a nightgown and coat, with curlers in her hair. 'What are you doing here?' Elizabeth asked.

'I don't know', the woman answered.

'My name is Elizabeth', said our friend. 'What's yours?'

'Clarity', replied the woman.

Meditative Reflection

All that is, is everywhere.
All that is surrounds and envelopes.
All that is is available in the sanctuaries and the wild.
For all that is simply is.

Chapter 3
Being all you can

The who, what, when, where, and why of spirit

Spirit, we are told, brings vitality to the combination of body-mind-soul – the wholeness of human experience. To date, body, mind, and soul have been the key characters in this text. We now introduce the lead element: spirit. The freedom to float and the power to impact on the human instrument makes spirit both a colourful and worthwhile subject. Spirit is the non-physical aspect of our being that comes into play when we have developed an awareness that our person goes beyond the parts of us that are made up of muscle and tissues. Spirit comes into to play when we connect with the fullness of all life and all living beings. It does not have a physical container and is able to move freely between the different levels of consciousness. Acting as the guiding principle of conscious life, spirit animates the body and mediates between body and soul. It functions outside the realm of day-to-day activities and daily concerns.

Spirit is the aspect of us that soars, unfettered by earthly concerns.
Spirit is a guiding principle of conscious life, animating body and mediating between body and soul.

Free spirit

The unfettered spirit, our guiding light to the why in our essence, connects our physical fundamentals to our intrinsic soul part. Soul is part of us. Spirit always allows us to have the soul viably interact with our physical dimension in order to express itself with a deeper underpinning to our mundane interactions.

In order to fully express oneself in the world as a caring, charitable, non-judgemental entity, we demand the dexterity spirit brings.

Through curiosity, focus on experimentation with our creative part, spiritual mobility, activity, and questioning, we test the borders of our creative potential. We can reach the heavens liberated from material and physical constraints; we are free to roam in the realm of inspiration.

– *The place where beauty, poetry, and music dwells*
– *The place where exploration brings forth more*
– *The place where sharing is gaining and limitations are nonexistent*
– *The place that frees our thinking and teaches us to look at our world with empathy and feeling*

Spirit's role as a font of the creative process puts a further twist on its potential function. Unencumbered by limited thinking and the mundane tasks of daily life, spirit is freed. This freedom enables it to bypass limitations through the sheer delight of creativity, and it affords us another very effective means of breaking up old patterns of both thinking and behaving. Using the word 'font', derived from 'fountain' and used to describe a baptismal basin, almost gives a religious connotation to the creative, or it can be seen as a well or fountain from which to draw.

Timing

Just when I thought the font was dry,
Words burst through the gate.
I thank you for these lines, Great Muse,
But must they come so late?

In all our writings, spirit got the 'big billing'. This vital role needed scrutiny. When we are told body is the vehicle, mind is the driver, and soul is the infuser, we thought we had a simple, well-functioning framework. The subsequent writings gave us an insight into spirit's functioning: unfettered by earthly constraints, powering the interaction and function of this powerful threesome.

Spirit as barometer

The team, with their unique and often playful way of stating things, refers to spirit as a barometer. Moving like a float on the water, spirit dips and bobs as it realigns and rebalances our body and mind with our soul levels. Why does this kind of adjustment make spirit so critical? Because body and mind must be operating in optimal balance in order for the integration of our soul level to function properly, spirit is constantly working as ballast, facilitating this alignment. Spirit could be acknowledged as the director or prime mover.

Operating unfettered or outside of earthly concerns allows spirit the freedom and flexibility to realign and rebalance the functions of the other members of the triad: body, mind, and soul. Like a float on an oil can, it is a reflective barometer of how connected the organism is to its deeper levels of functioning – a gauge of harmony. This relationship and the vitality of their relatedness are tantamount to the well-functioning of the total human system.

Spirit: the 'why'

Mind-spirit relationship is on the next scale of the decision-making process. As part of our complex system, it can be compared with the command centre. This is the area and part of us that decides 'why'.

> *Spirit is the part of us that decides why;*
> *our mind decides how, and our body does.*

The criterion for a well-integrated person is the full interaction of this triad within oneself and the ability to attain emotional and physical growth and well-being. The contentment and confidence of being able to function to the fullest within the confines of our life cycles and within the demands of our surroundings eliminates much debility, supporting this integrative process. Through acknowledgement of spirit, we eliminate the need for constant rededication and can then proceed to rethink the area of physical functioning and its implications.

Science has brought us the rewards of precise knowledge of the physiological relationship between the mind-body function. Pavlov's experiments with the salivation of dogs through triggering the imaginary processes were the beginning of great research in this area. The responses activated within the body through stimuli are a vast area of interest. Biofeedback techniques, backed by measurable evidence, have been able to activate these deliberately stimulated responses within the organism.

Emotional and spiritual satisfaction and ease have bearing upon our physical functioning. We ignore the idea of life cycles and karmic circumstances – and then we ponder the effects of emotional gloom upon the important area of physical functioning.

This interrelationship in relation to stress and the implications of the mind-body connection is explored further in chapter one, Identifying the Main Players – body-mind-spirit-soul.

In this whole mechanism, patterning is of great importance. Patterns can refer both to the repetitive behaviours, which have developed in our present life, or those which we have brought with us from former existences. These behaviours and traits can be readily seen in the personality frame within which we are born. How could we otherwise explain the distinctions so evident as one baby lies beside the other, each so differently?

This example of the differences in newborns clearly alludes to the reality of previous existences. The babies differ because they come into this life with specific characteristics and talents already in place.

The conscious smoothing out of connecting channels between the various components – body-mind, mind-spirit, spirit-body – clarify an understanding of the processes and a sense of awareness and perseverance that are important. Some refer to this as the opening of the third eye.

Self-sourcing – a beginning

This section begins to move us more deliberately into a practicing mode, with tools given for the process of self-sourcing.

> *The body is the sensor,*
> *the mind is the thought process,*
> *and the soul brings peace.*

Proper function of the body-mind in relation to the spirit depends on the vibrational level of each of the three components being compatible with each other. Each component has its individual needs to which they must both heed and adapt. Honing these parts involves integration and exercise for the body, feeding and learning for the mind, and peace of mind and body for the soul.

Assuming that the body-mind is working to its fullest potential and interacting at the optimum capacity, their mutual interactions and responsibilities will give the person a very viable, earthly vehicle. The transmission of the Self of the soul onto the substance of this vehicle is dependent upon the allowance of freedom given to the body-mind interaction. The integrative Self, sometimes called the third eye, has to be opened to allow this connecting point.

The necessary knowledge to function well in our chosen environment, in combination with viable and appropriate nutrition, is at the base of existence. It is asking too much of our bodies to expect them to function well over the long-term without access to the necessary nurturing at all levels.

The interaction of mind and body with the soul is acquired through awareness of the mind together with the subduing of the vibrational frequency of the body as our earthly vehicle. This is achieved through spiritual discipline.

The exercises for the mind and body are in a certain sense quite similar. The mind has first to stop and to listen; the strenuous part is the discipline of meditation. Regularity and frequency allow the mind to conquer strain and thus gain through achievement.

What has been provided above is an inventory of the necessary accomplishments in honing the functions of body and mind and bringing them to the proper vibrational frequency, where they can interact more freely with spirit.

Mind integration can be properly achieved through mind deployment. The mind is not a vehicle; it is a critical, self-governing focus of the self, the disciple of awareness. Judgemental aspects of our awareness – left brain versus right brain – captivate the non-judgemental Self of the soul. Meditation is the retreat from calculation and the emptying of the self. Only the empty vessel can be refilled. In doing this, allow yourself the enjoyment of a positive environment. Put sorrow where it belongs, but also put happiness in its place. The rhythms need to interact and can do so without any interference.

Alignment of body and mind into a combined pattern can be achieved by the exercise of both the physical and mental capacities: the body aligned and brought into balance, the mind attuned achieved through specific exercises. The result will be the synchronization of these two elements of physical functioning. Without the hocus-pocus of far earlier influences, we have brought down the emotions to a level of self-sourcing. Mudra (position), mantra (sound), and mandala (imagery), the three traditional Buddhist ways of focusing into the self, are tailor-made to instant Western patterning.

Watch the pebble,
listen to the sea.

At this point, the book takes a turn. Until now, much time has been spent laying a foundation of understanding. Who are the main players? What are the meanings of terms such as spirit and soul? We now move into the practical. How do we reach the lesser-known dimensions?

What sort of preparatory work is necessary? We had come to admire all of the components that make us into a viable entity. How, we asked, could we leave the seduction of exploring the spiritual unknown and live within a space where our foot stays solidly on the ground as we move into the endless dimensions?

Sound complicated? Not at all: the primary message is to make use of what surrounds us.

Exercise: a meditative walk

When laying out a garden, consider placing the stepping-stones just beyond the distance of a normal step. This forces you to slow down as you step from stone to stone, to bring the foot that lags behind to beside the one that leads. Initially this could prove irritating and somewhat of a challenge. None of these practices came easily to us; when we first tried to walk on irregular ground, we stumbled like anyone else. And certainly our first tries at meditation had us often doing grocery lists in our minds instead of reaching those touted realms of relaxation and emptiness. What was required was perseverance. In some ways it was easier for Gerbrig because she was already at ease with the contemplative, and she built a meditative pathway in her garden. It was many years before I had a sacred space constructed for my place of personal retreat. However, repetition and practice forces a slowing down and eventually places you into a slower, rhythmic pace, which is noticeably different.

As this sense of something different takes over, there is a tendency to look around, finding that time and pace are altered and have expanded into a meditative place. If the path is created in a winding way, it builds the elements of surprise and happenstance, thus enhancing the whole exercise of experiencing something different – an unobtrusive and painless way of entering into a meditative state. This idea is often integrated into Zen gardens.

What is the usefulness of this exercise? The walk incorporates mudra, albeit a moving one. Through the irregularity of the stepping stones and the focused awareness it requires us to have in order to do so such a walk, our logical mind is put on hold. We are forced to accept the unexpected. We were intrigued by the phrase 'the hocus-pocus of faraway influences'. This warning from our team deliberately steered us away from far-flung pursuits like regression, the search for soul mates, spoon bending, and table tipping. It clearly indicated that to achieve our grounding, our present status was still important. Were we being encouraged to clean our nest before stepping further?

This joyful little poem reminds us that beauty and silence can be found in the mundane. The hermit demonstrates the results when we 'test the borders of our creative potential'.

Insight

> *The blessed grin roams*
> *Upon the hermit's face.*
> *He meditates to keep in shape,*
> *Focuses in pure Taoist line*
> *On what the world would know*
> *As an old McDonald sign.*

Chapter 4
The whole in one

Achieving our fullest potential

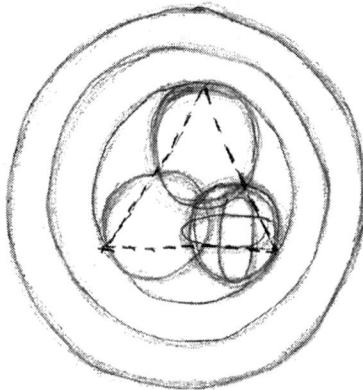

The sentence 'Achieving our fullest potential' is in actuality the essence of the book. The phrase itself is imbedded in the writing that follows. The stage is set, the players are identified, and you already have some exercises to slow you down, calm the mind, and release the chatter of everyday life. Now it's time to start putting it all together. Step up the pace. Though exercises have been provided in the introductory chapters, they will play a much more central role. Begin living to your fullest potential, with body, mind, spirit, and soul an integrated whole. But how?

How? Mind your mind

Mind-body approach

Again and again we remind that body is the vehicle, mind is the driver, and soul is the infuser. Spirit is a guiding principle of conscious life, animating body and soul. In essence this concept is the leading working principle in our effectiveness as a soul-inspired, joyful human being.

Again and again, as we look at the body-mind-spirit-soul, we see how each has its own function and consider how they interact. We would like to meditate now on the entity functioning within and with this deliberate and complex configuration. We know that body and its function is something we share with all living things. We ponder this entity with its complexity and moral underpinnings, combined with one's search for a spiritual meaning to its creation.

We often mentioned the mind being the driver. We extend this thought by saying that mind is, in effect, your creator. The extent of one's being is the deliberateness by which we determine the way we are. We live within and through our mindset, creating our own scenario; we are in essence our own masters.

Living within an integrated body-mind-spirit-soul can be said to be living to the fullest and in the full range of our own potential. This short phrase is the essence of this chapter and of the book itself. *Uncharted Corners of Consciousness*, as stated in its title, is a how-to guide for personal and spiritual growth. The goal of becoming a more fully developed individual moving towards enlightenment is about having our physical and non-physical parts in full play.

Trying to expand the understanding of the self and its many layers, we cannot help but look at avenues that will expand the function of our complex system.

How? Notice how mind affects body

Psychosomatic

With the advent of the twentieth century came a curiosity and interest in the whole area of the mind's affect on the body. This has only intensified as we move into the twenty-first century. Referred to as the psychosomatic approach, today we are likely to call it the mind-body connection – a term that suggests it is available to us on a personal level. 'Psyche' means 'of the mind', and 'soma' means 'of the body', so the psychosomatic approach is synonymous with the mind-body approach. This approach acknowledges that our thoughts have the ability to impact the body's well-being either positively or negatively. Prior to Candice Pert's discovery of the amino acids and research into how thoughts translate into chemical states in the body, psychosomatic had a negative connotation. It implied that a person was imagining their dis-eases and diseases. Now the mind is seen as a powerful ally in the healing process. The Simontons demonstrated the power of positive imagery to aid in healing cancer research. This whole area is discussed more fully a bit later in the chapter. Knowing that we have the ability to self-source is a comforting thought in this overinformed, overstimulated world. Aberdeen and Naisbett, in their 1986 book *Reinventing the Corporation*, state this so aptly: 'We are drowning in information and starved for knowledge'. To be able to tap into this pool of self-healing or rebalancing through techniques that act in a preventative way is an invaluable resource. Also, within the treatment fields all kinds of healing approaches have developed that encompass the understanding of the powerful impact that the mind-body feedback loop can have.

Current research regarding immunity and its connection to the physiological processes has brought us to understand the consequences of despair and stress on the functioning of our internal human regulator.

How? First accept that we are in a finite body and need to care for it

Our finite being

As physical units, we are at the mercy of a life cycle based on various levels of physical growth, maturation, and deterioration. Functioning within this cycle, we need to adapt to our varying personal capacities and abilities.

External factors and self-induced conditions present us challenges with which we are required to cope. They are the varieties and challenges of living.

Stress and anxiety imposed on us are the results of daily interaction with our environment. Immediately dealing with these is both exhilarating and depleting, mainly affecting us to the degree with which we relate to them.

This writing acknowledges that our environment will present us with a variety of stressors, whether event based or environmentally based. What makes the difference in whether we emerge enhanced or depleted depends on our personal interpretations.

> *There is nothing good or bad, but thinking makes it so.*
> – William Shakespeare, *Hamlet*

How? Examine your deepest feelings and strive for balance

Proper integration: constant motion

In order to function and to deal with ourselves within our total capacity, we must interrelate with our deepest feelings and contentions. Whatever may trigger us, it is our clear relationship with ourselves at the level of deepest meaning that should enable us to make decisions on a non-egotistical, discriminating level. This non-judgemental, non-evaluating property allows the caring motives to come into our functioning and decision-making: a straightforward, non-role-playing attitude giving everyday life a different meaning. Proper integration, be it physical or psychological, is constant motion. We can only strive to facilitate optimum balance.

This writing suggests that when we work on our deeper levels of awareness, we will automatically be more discerning and less judgemental. Given that we are bombarded with feelings good and bad, we have the ability to move from moods of deep despair or to exalted elation. The constant stretching and expanding of our consciousness leads to greater elasticity in our responses and enables us to have the emotional strength to ride out the times of stress. For example, your children or spouse arrive home with unexpected dinner company, and you still have an unfinished paper that is due the following day, and the cat is climbing up your newly hung curtains. Instead of sliding into a state of panic or confusion, by having practiced retreat into a place of detached observation – and what Gerbrig calls her "emotional safe haven" – you will have the ability to watch the events and ride their wave without getting snagged into a reactive place. Invariably the events themselves seem to magically fall into a place of order and ease.

The concept of taming the ego, or putting ego in its place, has come out from under its monk-like wraps and become au currant with many a popular figure. Long taught in Buddhist practice and led by the Dalai Lama, its new promoters Oprah Winfrey and Eckhart Tolle are endorsing the process, and their books are flying off the shelves. Throughout the writings they tout self-evaluation as essential. This is so masterfully taught by Byron Katie, leading us to enlightenment by examining our thoughts and questioning our assumptions. How lucky we were to have had a head-start as we worked with the writings some forty years ago.

How? Put ego in the backseat

Leaving ego behind

Precise guidance within a trusting and supportive relationship will clear the path for deep release within the emotional field. Myth and storytelling can then be omitted to evaluate events within the emotional hurt-field. Only then can the rebuilding of psychological health and vigour be started. Integrating the body-mind-spirit connection as part of the healing process can infuse fluidity.

One can achieve integration and meeting the need for soul-level experience by living life with opened eyes. The removal of ego-based functioning and the avoidance of goal orientation is disallowing; it does not allow the person to live life with unbiased, non-judgemental clarity.

Observing oneself moving away from the ego dimension allows the transcendental experience of contact on the soul level; when time stands still, future and past are one, and commitments drop.

A holistic approach is more than getting a tumour out of the stomach. It requires us to deal with our angers, grudges, hurts, and expectations and asks us to go deeper and heal them – to reach the point where we leave ego behind.

The Dalai Lama is a shining example of leaving ego behind and living a non-critical attitude of peacefulness and compassion. He even links our attitudes to our state of healthfulness: 'Feelings of anger, bitterness, and hate are negative; if I kept them inside me they would spoil my body and my health. They are of no use'.[2] When the Chinese exiled him from Tibet, instead of regarding them as his enemy, the Dalai Lama perceived the Chinese as a catalyst. Without them he would have remained an isolated monk in the mountains of Tibet; the Chinese sent him out into the world. When we do not integrate spirit and soul into our daily lives, it is exiling ourselves from the outside world. In addition to providing individual healing through changing one's attitude to adverse conditions, the Dalai Lama provides an opportunity for healing that has the potential to reach beyond the immediate and personal, to impact on more extensive and non-personal levels.

How? Examine and change your habitual behaviours

Undoing dysfunctional patterns

As a society seemingly addicted to fulfilling our pleasures, one could cite a number of situations of habitual behaviours that are self-destructive, from obesity to gambling to sexual conquests. In our civilization, with its many advantages, one can all too easily be seduced by the lure of excess. Changing these patterned behaviours requires conscious awareness.

Habitual behaviours, with their established paths, demand facing them as hindrances to be overcome. The deconditioning of a feature is turning it around and strengthening it into a new and positive response. Recognition of deconditioning is an important approach to the one seeking to effect change.

---

[2]   Margaret Gee, *Words of Wisdom from the Dalai Lama: Quotes by His Holiness*, New York: Gramercy Books, 2005, 33.

Repeating occurrences of physical deficiencies in certain areas of our body are clues to which it resorts.

A Visit Home

She sees through filtered eyes,
Hears through muffled ears.
Her world has shrunk;
The change is obvious.
She places things in specified spots,
Seeking to keep her mind in order.
As I watch, expectations fade.
I see myself in her.

Utilizing a holistic approach

A holistic approach searches for answers within the interrelationships of body, mind, and soul. It seeks to unearth the root causes of disease rather than treat symptom alone by examining the full picture that surrounds the disease pattern. In this process the mind becomes an equal player and ally in the diagnostic and treatment scenario.

In our personal search for holism and healing, we found that often holistic therapies could unearth answers not always provided by Western medicine. The drawings and our entire course of study came about because of our search into unanswered questions. Sometimes the information simply built on the medical findings, giving an added view or perspective. Sometimes they unearthed findings which were missed, left unaddressed, or were completely unavailable from conventional channels. The 'multidimensional faceting' mentioned in the writing refers to the many aspects of the Self.

Multidimensional faceting requires the depth of multifaceted insight.

Modern medicine, with its tremendous advantages, treats symptoms at the physical level with great accuracy. Scientific knowledge and technology in modern Western life has increased life expectancy and has done much to enhance human comfort.

With the growth of new developments in medical science came the evolution of methodologies, including the awareness of our psyche and its influence on physical well-being. This deeper understanding of the root of unconscious that functions on the psychological know-how broadens one's scope greatly. Alternative health care embraces this approach, including the deeper soul level as an integral part of treatment.

The holistic approach

There are many therapies and holistic approaches one could seek as tools for integrating body, mind, spirit, and soul. Several of them stand out, and their innovators present as stars or giants in their field. We will give some of them brief mention in this chapter, and their bodies of work will be expanded upon in the application chapters in the later part of the book.

We must add a caveat: there are many others practitioners who are equally capable and whose work is laudable. This list is by no means comprehensive but rather is a rich sampling chosen because those mentioned are the methodologies with which we worked most extensively.

Bodywork and visualization both can serve as avenues for the integration of body and mind. When used together, the interaction of bodywork and visualization stand a greater chance of allowing for spirit to come forward into consciousness. Attention to both the mind and the body is what a holistic approach is truly all about.

One effective form of bodywork is Trager, named after its founder, the late Dr Milton Trager. Dr Trager realized that the state of the practitioner could activate a response in the client; the mind could affect a chemical change in the body. The Trager method uses gentle rocking on a massage table to effectively bore the active mind. This facilitates access of the unconscious, where unneeded patterns are stored and can be released. Trager differs from regular massage in that it uses no oils and is not directed towards fixing anything. Rather it offers a pleasurable experience to the client that replaces the uncomfortable and negative patterns formerly experienced. The new way of feeling and being is then reinforced when off the massage table by simple movements called 'mentastics', mental gymnastics, and this anchors and establishes the new patterns of comfort and ease. Milton Trager's phrase, 'How should it be?' so accurately describes the healing power of his technique; people return to a state of functioning or comfort, which is how they should have been all along. Audrey Mairi, Jack Liston, and Cathy Guadagno, in concert with Milton Trager himself, provide much additional information on the origins and use of this powerful healing method,[3] while Deane Juhan explores and explains the physiology behind the effective outcomes of Trager.[4]

Dr. Carl Simonton and his wife, Stephanie Matthews-Simonton, are well-respected authors in the field of visualization. The Simontons use visualization extensively when treating cancer patients. Their work emotionally empowers patients to be active participants in their healing process. One of their best-known images casts cancer as a hamburger and the white blood cells as Pac-Men gobbling up the tumours.

The effect that focused thinking has on our physiology has been widened once again, thanks to the work of Dr Candace Pert, former director of the brain biochemistry division at the National Institute of Mental Health. Dr Pert is known for her work in identifying how vital the neuropeptides molecules are in understanding the conversation taking place between body and mind. We have come to know that the brain and body are in a constant feedback loop. We now know that the body can think.

In 1978, Dr Hans Selye, a Canadian endocrinologist of Austrian Hungarian descent, was a front runner in the field of mind-body approach and its relationship to stress management. He enabled us to develop an insight into the sequence of events whereby both stress – and anxiety-related symptoms can suppress the immune processes within the body. He saw that correlations could be drawn between these events and the onset of major disease.

---

[3]   Trager, M., Guadagno, C. (1988), *Trager mentastics: movement as a way to agelessness*, Barrytown, NY: Station Hill Press; Liskin, J., (1996), *The life and work of Milton Trager, MD*, Barrytown, NY: Station Hill Press; Mairi, A. (2006), *Trager for self-healing: a practical guide for living in the present moment*, H. J. Kramer Books.

[4]   Juhan, D. (1987), *Job's Body: a handbook for bodywork*, Barrytown, NY: Station Hill Press.

Dr Herbert Benson taught that using a repetitive thought or mantra could break the self-perpetuating stress cycle. Through his books and subsequent research at Harvard, he moved this kind of thinking and practice into the public domain.

Dr Norman Cousins brought laughter and positive thinking into his treatment programs. Cousins encouraged us to examine our patterns and habitual behaviours to ensure that they are supportive and non-destructive to our well-being. He warned that people have a tendency to repeat their patterns. 'Habits', he cautioned, 'are first cobwebs and then cables'.

Dr Sandra Seagal conducted in-depth research into the development of people from the beginning of life as specific whole systems of mental-emotional-physical interplay, (mental, emotional, and physical having both personal and transpersonal dimensions). Each of these human systems, or 'ways of being', is characterized by its own distinctive processes of experiencing experience, taking in and assimilating information, learning, experiencing and expressing emotion, communicating and relating with others, experiencing stress, and maintaining wellness. Each is also characterized by its own distinctive path of personal, interpersonal, and transpersonal integration and development.

Understanding these distinctions in people's inherent make-up enables people to harmoniously accommodate one another's systemic processes and to fulfil their individual and collective potential. Because the patterns are there from the beginning of life, human dynamics is especially valuable for educators and parents and is invaluable for those working in health care and human development.

It would be an oversight if we didn't mention the many Eastern disciplines that have established themselves in the Western world, filling a gap in the search for integration of body and mind and finding holism. Several individuals can be credited with bringing these longstanding Eastern disciplines to the Western world. One example Maharishi Mahesh Yogi and TM (transcendental meditation). He brought meditation to the forefront, and it was further popularized by his association with the Beatles and his presence at Woodstock. Today, meditation has penetrated mainstream in multiple variations, including the now popular practice of yoga, which is sweeping the West, and the moving meditative disciplines of tai chi and chi gong and NIA. The list goes on.

Disciplines of mind and body through various martial arts, long ago the purview of yogis alone, have now made its way into the public domain. They have been popularized through such Hollywood personalities as Steven Segal and Jackie Chan, and even in the world of animation, such as *Kung Fu Panda* (Osborne & Stevenson, 2008). Acupuncture, which works with the meridians and biofeedback, has also established a firmer foot hold in conventional treatments.

The body and its responses

Repetition is the body's most powerful way of learning, be it babies learning to walk or adults learning to play a sport or instrument. When the body is injured, the familiar way of doing things is ended, and so it sets up new patterns to facilitate healing. A leg won't let you walk; an arm will have a limited range of movement. Perhaps a stroke victim will need to learn to write with their non-dominant hand. Over time, these coping mechanisms become established patterns. You know where to find the light switch in a dark room. The problem is that when the healing has taken place through such things as physiotherapy, people are still left with the automatic actions associated with their injured patterns. These memories are there because the unconscious mind is still holding onto that memory, and the memory is embedded in the muscles themselves. Today the term 'muscle memory' is well recognized. What has to happen is a conscious awareness and reinforcement of the new patterns of movement, like relighting a fire or turning on a light switch. Then this new pattern must be reinforced. The writing goes on to highlight some of the retriggering tools.

Repeated triggering of certain responses within the body will eventually lead to an established pathway for the thought-and-functioning process. Certain sounds, smells, sights, and feelings will trigger responses thought long forgotten. The fight-or-flight response, activated on a forgotten level, can become aggravated and evoke negative responses when resistance is low.

Many forms of holistic therapies, with the deeper sensitivity they use, have the ability to bring forth remnants of physical responses long forgotten, redirecting and deactivating whatever effects they might have had on the physical interaction. This becomes a redirection that becomes a redirection of nerve cell interaction on the muscular pattern. Through abnormal stimulation of the muscular tissue, the regular reference of time and space is disrupted, allowing withdrawal to points of recognition – the framework of our thought placed on our physical body.

Visualization, forming a mental image, and imagery are metaphorical methods through which we try to reach the symbolic coding that stores our memories. They are mind processes. Through visualization of an idealized state, we direct the mind to recognize certain circumstances. Through repetition of a detailed information pattern, the responses will establish conditions for a gateway into a new functioning process.

Recall

Crisp blue sky,
Bold sunlight,
Miles of virgin ice
Swept clean as by a giant broom
Awaiting the intrusion of our blades.
Unknown the bounds of manmade rinks;
Unconfined, we skate.
The fire draws us to its warmth.
All remembered as I hear your song.

In the previous writings, we explored the vast abilities contained within the body-mind feedback loop. The withdrawal to points of recognition mentioned in the writing alludes to what a Trager session addresses. The abnormal stimulation which it describes is a continuous, repetitive rocking so different from massage. We saw how visualization can hold us in a place of fear and failure, or create conditions for comfort and success. Further, we learned the importance of bringing things to the conscious level of awareness to ensure we were not caught in a web of habitual behaviour. To initiate and stimulate the healing process, a person must first understand what factors produce the damaging stress reaction.

When Shelly broke her pelvis in an automobile accident, during her healing journey she first had to identify what behaviours might have led to such an event. She realized that her stress was caused by rushing, lack of focus, emotionally upsetting events, and putting the demands of others above herself. Once these factors were understood, she could incorporate strengthening behaviours and visualization patterns into recovering. Visualization was a major partner in her recovery and along with homeopathics, energy work, ultrasound, and cranial sacral work, her bone was healed in six weeks rather than twelve.

Olympians provide us with the most encouraging example of positive mental imagery. If they reinforced their fearful and jittery responses they have prior to competing in their events, they would damage their chances. But what they do is see themselves winning as they train for competitions. That is how winners are made! Only through such conscious recognition can new patterns of response be worked out and accepted by the person. Recognition of the stress syndrome and evaluation of its causes and their contributing circumstances can redirect and rechannel the person's unproductive and harmful response patterns into a healthier approach.

Finally, we learn that the more we are able to develop a flexibility of functioning – one where we access our uncharted corners of consciousness – the greater chance we have of extending beyond the limitations of the body to enter the realm of the spirit and perhaps unity with all that is.

How? Prepare the conditions for the soul to flourish!

Treading the uncharted corners of consciousness

Spirit and soul deal with a nomenclature relating to a capacity from within. Mind, social interaction. and the ability to function within a society are ego-based. Soul is universally based, a depth of caring, understanding, and love which does not turn its back on the human, but sees it as a small part of the total.

Working with the concept that the body is a thought manifest of the spirit, we see the body as a tool for the mind. Thought manifest is soul as it chooses to express itself into physical form through thought. Knowing this informs us that body and mind are a working partnership in allowing the soul to flourish. In essence this assures us that problems we might have with bodily issues can enrich us at a soul level. If we work with them in a positive, mindful way, anything can be seen as learning.

Body and mind are channelled into a purpose of which the spirit, our link with the universe, is the maker.

When we achieve a total person who is able to evaluate his emotional responses to the outside world, we can start to rechannel his emotional responses to himself. Enjoyment of functioning within a world that feels compatible makes us feel compatible and able to act accordingly.

Functioning physically and emotionally to maximum capacity is a challenge. Excitement about life and living, in totality, is responding appropriately and functioning to the fullest.

Opening up the concept of mind-soul invariably results in giving a deeper meaning and intention to the issues at hand. The consideration is that the deeper Self, the intrinsic transitory vehicle, is on a basic, superconscious, indifferent power level. It is neither good nor bad; it just is. It is a mode of breathing energy within the life span to which one is committed, with the purpose of serving the aim of perfection of the entity.

With the aim of perfection, the higher Self aspect of the body-mind-spirit relationship is then geared to being good, caring, and loving. The basic intrinsic Self of each of us should be and is in the realm of good. Soul can be seen as the nerve cell tuned to its high aspirations: a translator of a far-away impulse, an apparatus of function.

Each of body, mind, and soul has its function on a higher hierarchical level, translating a mode that is higher than itself to a level of functioning, which will broaden its total scope.

Access to divinity is through our soul or spirit. Acceptance of spirit, soul within the self, and nurturing our connection and dependence on and with this abstract part of us needs the clarity and function of a mind not impeded by a burdened physical. Deep meditation, which has at its core a clearing of the mind, functions as an access to the soul, the centre of our being – a window. It allows an arrival of a purpose based on the very highest level.

Attention to the self requires a honing. Depending on the activity, it reaches towards the level to which it is scaled, the succession or progression of steps or degrees, and the ranking of importance. Deeper interaction with the self on a spiritual level determines the level of functioning of the total Self. Deep interaction with the mind concerns the mind and the physical. Purely physical interaction is an area of visual recognition. In the field of the obvious, it is where it can be seen.

The reaching of the deeper Self will follow the opposite pattern. In order to get to this inner core within each of us, we could compare it with the unpeeling of layers. The careful wrappings we carry are to be peeled one by one. Needs should be taken care of and satisfactions granted.

To discuss soul level with a hungry man is the ballroom dancing of the lame.
We function to answer our destiny, regardless of our circumstances.
We choose our route!
Phlegmatic acceptance of one's fate is one thing,
but searching for one's route and one's part in it is the other.

The initial part of this writing deals with the need for attaining balance within the emotional and physical realms as essential preparation for accessing soul level and, ultimately, integrating spirit. It assures us that one of the byproducts of this honing will be a clear understanding of our soul purpose.

A second byproduct is the extension of the person into the realm of total humanity – the arena of selfless service. Here we are pushed to look at the admonishment given to us about the hungry man whose interest in dancing is nonexistent. It clearly reminds us that we are responsible for our fellow man. This refers us back to the start of the writing, which gives import to our social interactions and our place as members of the society at large.

Later, we are told that access to the higher dimensions comes not from the level of mind or intellect, but rather from setting these functions aside. Ultimate respect is given to one's individual approach and to one's right to choose the how and when. This concept is reinforced with a cautionary note to therapists to do the same. Gerbrig's personal experience in this area happened more than forty years ago when, as a nurse, she was in a situation where her scientific training did not seem to solve the needs of a patient under her care. The patient could not be consoled and was a disruption to the ward and all the staff.

Frustrated, Gerbrig retreated to her office and closed the door to find a way to address the situation. She took some deep breaths and began to doodle, and when she looked down at her drawing, she was surprised. What she had drawn was a stick figure with a mastectomy, like the patient on the ward. Embarrassed, she scratched the drawing out, and the lines showed up as arms hugging the stick figure. Giving over to impulse, she went directly to the patient and put her arms around her. She told her she felt badly about her distress and asked how she could help. The woman eased more into Gerbrig's arms, started to cry, and thanked her for being there; she apologized for being so demanding and then told her story. Having lost all of her family in the Holocaust, and with all friends aged and unable to visit, she felt abandoned. 'All I needed was a hug', she said.

Gerbrig could hardly believe what she was hearing, and no one could have predicted the remarkable turn-around in the patient, who became communicative and cooperative. Having stepped out of her normal mode of functioning, Gerbrig had, to her great surprise, discovered an opening to a resource before unknown to her. She had stepped into another mode of functioning, a different level of awareness, one which was not a part of her everyday venues but provided her with a different relationship to herself and others. This dimension was inside of her – and it is inside each and every one of us.

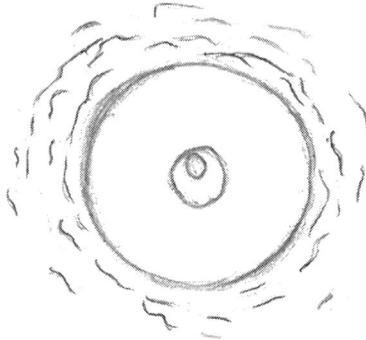

Using visualization to access the spirit

The following writing directs us on how to use visualization to gain access into the realm of spirit. It emphasizes focus and specificity as keys to success.

Visualization is a term used to describe clearly the needs and wants that one requires to access in a purposeful manner – a mouthful for the focus of a specific meditation.

In general, a meditation is used and needed to quicken the Self in its daily interactions as well as to free the inner self. A guided meditation or visualization is used to access and direct to specific needs. Assistance is requested from soul level; it is a request that asks for redirection of the highest level. The ability of soul to support is dependent on the range of functioning developed in the being. Meditation and visualization focuses on redirecting physical choices and emotional support. It is asking for redirection on the highest level.

Silence and clarity times three. In silence and clarity we direct ourselves. Meditation is the silence; visualization is giving direction in the clarity. The physical plane, in all its metaphors and senses, directs to its higher Self for a request for change. When our higher Self evidences, it does so in its own personal metaphor. We respond in a manner to which we are acquainted and direct ourselves accordingly.

A mere 'help' only gets one answer: 'With what?'

Exercise: relaxing up

Seat yourself in a comfortable position: arms and legs uncrossed, spine straight. Begin by closing your eyes and taking one or two deep breaths in and out. Pause a moment and instruct yourself that you will be assuming a position of alert relaxation. Proceed by focusing your attention on the sound of breathing in through your nose and out through your mouth. Do this several times.

Then, keeping your eyes shut, allow your attention to shift its focus onto your feet. Imagine that you are drawing up any tension you encounter as if it were a liquid pulled up through a straw. Pull it up from your feet, up through your legs, up the calves, and up the thighs; take all the tension you have gathered and let it rest in your belly. Shift your attention to your arms; draw up any tension up through your fingers, your forearms, your elbows, and your upper arm, and let all the tension you have gathered rest in your chest. Shift your attention to your head, from the tip of your chin to the top of your skull; draw up and tension in to the spot between your eyebrows. Draw in any sounds, smells, feelings, or tension and place them in that spot between your eyebrows. Now shift your attention back to your belly and pick up all of the tension you have there to gather it up into your chest. Then take all of the tension you have left in your chest and gather it up into the

43

spot between your eyebrows. Take a moment to scan your body and see if there is any tension left, and if there is, gather it up, draw it up through your body, and place it in that spot between your brows. Then focus your attention on the spot between your brows and take all of the attention you have gathered; imagine that you are releasing out from a space five or six inches above your head, and let it all cascade down. With your eyes closed:

- See yourself in a strong and healthy body that supports all you want to do
- See yourself with a mind that is clear and non-judgemental
- See yourself with a spirit that moves unencumbered by earthly concerns
- See yourself with viable soul that informs and infuses you

Now ask, 'What do I look like when my body, mind, spirit, and soul are functioning as a whole?' Let the answer present itself.

This exercise provides us with a focused and grounded vantage point, from a place of focused awareness rather than mind-driven wilfulness. We can ask for the help we need and move into integration and redirection on the highest level. Do not get discouraged if pictures and answers do not pop up immediately or provide instant illumination. Practice makes perfect and repetition is your ally. Achieving our fullest potential is a lifelong process and perhaps even beyond – but now we're skipping ahead; reincarnation is chapter six.

Three Men on a Crane

Human spiderman,
Perched in the heavens.
What magnetic force drew you to the clouds?
Did you forget you couldn't fly?

Chapter 5
The maturing soul

Soul infiltrates the everyday

This chapter is about the battle between the ego (self), whose job it is to glue us to the everyday with its dedication to acquisition, and the power of our higher Self and its emancipation from the mundane to the selfless spiritual place. It also uses the metaphor of physically growing up, sometimes said to be like shifting from one foot to the other.

There is a sequential movement to these writings that takes us deeper and deeper into engaging actively in the process of the unfolding of the soul: 'a series of thin slices of the self scrutinized and decoded'.

Finally, the self and Self come face-to-face in a duel for supremacy. As the soul moves from infancy to adulthood, the small self recedes, while the larger Self steps into its strength – planting us firmly on our spiritual legs. This is the foundation we will need as we stand in full partnership with creation itself and the struggle against good and evil. We do, however, continue to hop back and forth on both sets of legs, so that we can stand in our daily lives as we reach for the lofty realms.

The two sets of legs differentiate metaphorically between our Earth legs and spirit legs.

The concept of creation

In this writing, respect is given to various religious interpretations and storytelling; however, it does make a definitive link of the soul to the divine, emphatically so in the final sentence.

    'Concept of creation', the first writing in this chapter, speaks of the original casting of humans in the image of their divine origins. Finally, in 'The emergence of the soul', we encounter the involvement of the person in assisting this process of unfoldment of the soul.

The large, divine concept of creation is handed down to us through the spoken heritage and generally laid down within our scriptures. Through the metaphor of Adam and the paradise, we equate ourselves as the progenies of creation infused with G-d's breath. In the Judeo-Christian acceptance, it has been translated within tradition and the religious context as the accepted norm. In other civilizations, comparable belief systems are known to emphasize the human's affiliation for and descendency from a higher power. Nomenclature in this regard is as diverse as the range and versatility of our physical set-up allows. The soul as centre of the human being is cast in the image of its divine origin.

The soul and its implications

The exquisiteness of these writings is that they give credence to religion and our connectedness to a divine source of origin without boxing us into a particular belief system. Enlightenment within the Hindu tradition is alluded to, as is self-actualization in the Western world. We are warned not to get bogged down in nomenclature, yet we are told to realize that the subjectivity of our socio-cultural experiences does influence our belief system, as well as the verbal expression of those beliefs.

The discussion in this particular writing alerts us to the influence that socio-cultural conditions exert on our individual development.

Within the metaphysical context of our belief system, we find the many similarities within the thought process of the human being: the expression of the benign overpowering source of our being.

The assumption of our link with the transcendency of our being to an origin of creation depends on the subjectivity of our cultural and our social and religious background. Within the ethereal world of our conception, each of us will present a part of the G-d concept.

Gods – good or evil, devils or archangels – are the equations for the good versus bad concept. This raises the object level to assimilating the good or comforting against the bad, as represented by fear and anxiety as it manifests to us. A comfortable situation then becomes a homeostatic endeavour for which to aim.

Enlightenment within the Hindu tradition is the striving and finding and understanding one's original beginning and merging again with the G-d concept which was a part of one's creation. Life or loves, as seen through reincarnation, are the means of attaining perfection in order to return to the origin of casting (the creator).

Life as a learning process does show the depths of its multifaceted dimension and the perfection of its total, like the polishing of the stone in order to bring out the fullest dimension. The need for perfection then becomes the need for self-actualization through the maturing of the soul into an entity capable of being at one with, yet a viable and independent aspect of, the creator, beauty, and love.

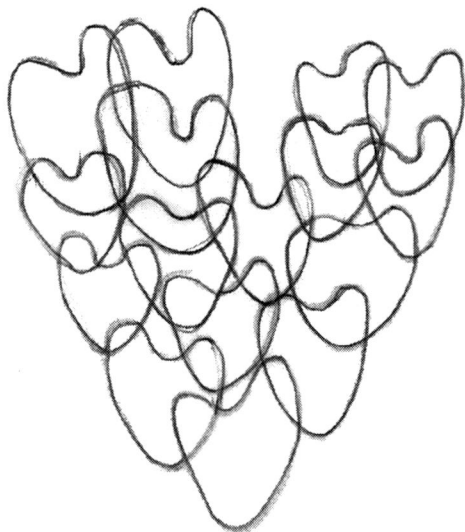

The emergence of the soul

In this writing, the word 'soul' is rarely used. In its place, we find the terms I, Self, spirit, everlasting essence, and spirituality. *The names depict the same essence of our being, the third dimension within our body-mind-soul concept.* We also acknowledge the purposefulness of the ego. It is seen as playing an important role in defining the self at a personality rather than a transpersonal level, balancing the body and mind so that the expression of the spirit can emerge.

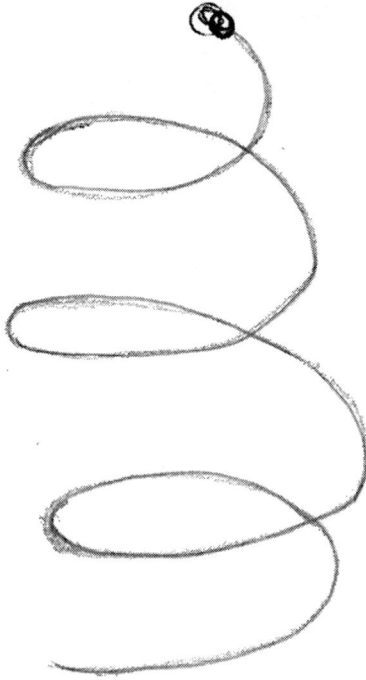

The emergence of the soul is the looking into the self and its workings – the knowledge of whence and where we came from.

The obliteration of the self and the demands of the ego and its needs is one-pointedness, which allows us the awareness to go into a dimension which is more the Self than the ego could ever be.

The focusing of the awareness into the universal energy and the understanding that one's beginnings is within the roots of creation is the merging of self with its divine purpose. The acknowledgement of the connection of spirituality in and of the self to the universe in its wholeness is knowledge of the renewal of the bond with the eternal Self.

The everlasting essence of Self transcending time and material allows for permanence, where the physical is transient; there is an awareness of allowing the spirit to grow through the levels of knowing and then applying the knowledge to fields of learning.

This is submitting to viewing one's life based on spiritual perpetuity, while allowing ego its place and its own demands. The ego is merely the vehicle, the carriage of our being whose purpose is absorption and a tooling of the self.

The benefits of meditation allow for the development and growth in the workings of the Self within a sphere of awareness. With one-pointedness as its aim, it frees the physical and its senses to focus on this aspect of the Self.

The goal is alignment of the physical and intellectual, body and mind, to be a receptacle so that the spirit can emerge. The vibrational frequency of the self is thus totally stilled so that the 'I' can speak; this is the maturing of the soul.

Reconciling everyday existence and soul life

This inspired message should be noted as the one that shifts the book into application. Given the necessary terminology, and with the stage set in terms of context, the reader is now invited to put these understandings to work. We are encouraged to pursue actively the integration of the mundane with the sacred, acknowledging the importance of both. We have been repeatedly astonished by the specificity of terminology used in these writings. This one is no exception. The term 'hi-fi', well known as 'high fidelity', could sound whimsical or archaic in today's age of information. Yet when we researched it through one of our favourite sources, the *Random House Dictionary*, and added the teachings of our team, we were once again humbled. Hi-fi in the vernacular, the world of records, is sound reproduction with a full range of audible frequencies. The copy has very little distortion from the original. In our text, hi-fi refers to our well-honed ability to receive information from the meditative realms where there are no words, and as we bring this through our personal filter, we must do so with as little distortion as possible. Thus, it can filter meaningfully into our lives.

Even the word 'propensity', used to describe accelerated understanding, has a specific slant. It is defined as 'a strong, often uncontrollable, natural inclination or tendency' (Random House, 2005). How familiar is this unexplainable pull to learn and to grow within the spiritual realm? Once the door is opened to seeking our reasons for being, it usually remains ajar. Next comes 'adhere', used when speaking of the three levels of body-soul-learning. Besides adhere's obvious meaning, 'to stick fast, as with glue', it also means 'to be a follower or upholder' or 'to hold firmly' (Random House, 2005) – strong reinforcement for the ultimate importance these three levels carry.

These definitions that challenged our thinking are not something we can dismiss easily, for often the more obscure explanations were the ones that most often dovetailed with the spirit-given material. They in turn jarred us and forced us to drop our previous notions. For example 'fidelity', unexpectedly used as a term for intuition, expanded our ordinary interpretations and augmented our field of awareness. We invite you to work with these concepts and recommend you give yourself latitude to explore a score of possible interpretations.

Messages and learning on this level are on a plane quite different than previously written. We enter now an arena where we have to look at functionality. Practicality and its every issue are hard to handle when focusing on soul level.

The underpinnings of a functioning body are soul. Deep and quiet understanding of oneself in space and time is essential. We have already dealt with this particular concept in previous writings.

Our aim is now to hone in on aspects of learning and functionality. We must bring intuitive knowledge with us and make it applicable – our 'hi-fi', so to say. We learned that body is unity: Unity of body-soul and learning. We have to focus in on the function of body-soul-learning.

Body has no future; it has a present presence, a focus in our total function, a part-time transportation. It simply is a self-destructing item.

Learning has the propensity of accelerating understanding of the functions of either body or soul. We have to understand the meaning of each (body, soul) so we can ask the 'why' and the 'how' and then do the latter (learn).

Application

Further within the sequence of the writing itself, we are given specific techniques for assisting the emergence of the soul. The team instructed us to follow these steps sequentially.

> 1. *Obliteration of the self and the demands of the ego*
> Setting a tone of relaxation is always a preparatory step to leaving the ego behind, and therefore the progressive relaxation from chapter two can be re used over and over again. Having done that exercise, proceeding to the exercise below will cover the three remaining points: universal focus, connection to universal wholeness, and transcending time and material. These exercises can become part of your personal practice.
> 2. *Focusing of the awareness into the universal energy*
> 3. *Acknowledgement of the connection to the universe in its wholeness*
> 4. *Transcending time and material*

Exercise: connecting with the universal energy

Visualize yourself sitting on a beach and facing the ocean. Feel the sand under your feet as you take note of your surroundings. Allow your eyes to connect with the sea; follow the waves rolling in to shore and out, over and over again. Breathe in through nose, and as you inhale, feel the relentless energy of the ocean entering and permeating your body. Breathe out through your mouth, and as you do, release your breath out into the sky, following the movement of your breath. Then as you inhale a second time, notice your breath as it re-enters and infuses your body, pulling the vitality of the ocean with it. This time on the exhale, as you release your breath, let it extend all the way out to the stars. Repeat this cycle of drawing the universal energy into your being as you inhale through your nose and extending out into the universe as you exhale through your nose. Allow yourself to dissolve into this endless circle of energy of which you are a part, and acknowledge your connection to the universe in its wholeness. Offer thanks for being a part of all this expansive beauty. When you are ready to disconnect once again, notice the sand beneath your feet and feel strengthened, refreshed, and acutely aware of where you stand. From this place of thankfulness and clarity, slowly open your eyes and, holding on to your connection to the universal, become aware of your physical surroundings.

These writings once again reinforce the importance of meditation as a tool for achieving focus and one-pointedness – a means of meeting the deeper Self.

Growth

The going on in essence
Is acquiring what was not,
And teaching to the self
That perpetuity never ends;
Allowing one the lesson
Of working on the self –
Which does need perfecting,
Only on its new level.

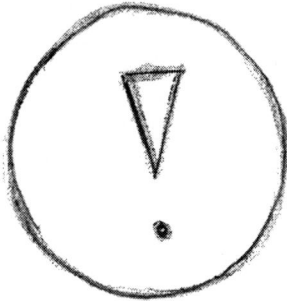

Worthiness and response, ability

If in essence we see ourselves as a worthwhile personage, with a past and a present, we do have to answer to a viability and worthiness. Seeing with clarity our own place within the creation concept, we will also have to answer to our need to fill a space within it, which is worthy to our feeling of Self.

Man and woman have the ability to deal with basic concepts: black is wrong and white is right, going forward is good and going backward is bad. To be able to grab life and its implications, joys, and demands is to fulfil one's soul-dream.

Longing

I just want to feel real love,
Fill the home that I live in.
And I just want to feel real love
And a life ever after.
There is a hole in my soul.
You can see it in my face;
It's a real big place ...

This small writing embraces several key issues: worthiness, viability, self-actualization, and soul-dream. It begins with the use of the term 'personage', a person of distinction or importance. What a strong message of personal empowerment! The teachings go on to express how essential this feeling of self-importance can be to the eventual acceptance of responsibility on a soul level for the fulfilment of one's soul-dream. The tone of the writing, reflected in such words as 'grab life and its implications', holds an exuberance and strength. It emphasizes the importance of a strong concept of the personal self in finding one's place of comfort and purpose within the totality of creation.

This has very important therapeutic implications. It reinforces the fact that how one views his or her own self has great impact on how one shapes one's life – an encouraging point of view for reframing and reshaping a life and its purpose. Do you see the glass as half-empty or half-full? This makes an important case for strengthening the ego for a sturdy sense of self-worth, establishing a stable platform for the leap into the search for spiritual fulfilment. This perspective is not always emphasized in spiritual practices that strive more for the obliteration of the ego. Those who have read this book sequentially will recognize two familiar notes and recurrent themes of this collection of teachings: the essential need for positive thinking and the vast respect given to personal choice.

We have chosen to end this chapter on the maturing soul with this meditative poem. We must take full responsibility for our own self-development. Contained within is the duality of protecting and guarding oneself while being willing to step outside this protective space and dare to share what one knows. Remember the need for appreciation and thanksgiving, for optimism, and for the availability of the mysteries of body and soul to all.

No Props

And then it stopped.
I was given no pictures,
No aids,
No tracks to reach the Self.
I knew I was the Self.

Chapter 6
Reincarnation

Life is only one edition? Cancel my subscription!

Reincarnation, the rebirth of the soul in a new body, has always been a part of cultural thinking, religious writings, and oral history, although it has not always been universally accepted. In essence, we are dealing with a belief system equally divided among believers and agnostics, much the same as the sphere within which belief in a God falls.

In the latter part of the twentieth century, people rejuvenated interest in reincarnation as medical science reported more 'back from the dead' death events and 'into the light' stories. The curiosity continued as people asked, 'Is death really final?'

Previous life regressions, though subjective, presented a viable case for the continuity of life after death. Reincarnation supports the notion of a transpersonal aspect of the self, answering to the need for a meaning to our present-life existence.

Over the years, we received many writings on this subject – some in response to our own questions; others in reply to requests from others. Many times the material was given without our asking at all. There were times when we might have been discussing a particular topic, trying to find an appropriate definition for a word or explanation of a concept over which we were disagreeing. Suddenly both of us would feel an 'aha' and knew that the team had a point of view to share; we would stop, get out a piece of paper, and start writing. When finished we compared our writings. Always the information was the same, but given that it had gone through our individual, personal filters, the style of writing varied. In those situations, it was clear to us that our learning was being deliberately guided, and instinctively we knew the team taught us important lessons.

Because we are merely the vehicles through which this information flows, we took a willing step back for this particular chapter. We let the writings do their own talking. You will see fewer explanations, and we will invite you to bring your own responses and interpretations into them. However, given we are the mediums of these messages, we will insert certain comments if we feel they offer clarification or help raise questions.

As much as anyone, we remain intrigued by the questions, 'Who are we?' and 'What is the purpose of our existence?'

Never forget that life is lived in the present ...

Reincarnation?

The idea of the maturing soul travelling through subsequent incarnations has been a controversial matter of self-search and research alike. The probability of the soul's enduring nature is a vast subject appealing to many beliefs and integrated philosophies; it is championed and disclaimed with equal intensity.

Recent acceptance of the life-after-death phenomenon and actively triggered past-life regression has added a modern version to religious, philosophical, and metaphysical beliefs about the nature of the soul.

Consideration that the spiritual part of us does survive gives us food for thought. It challenges us to accept that its existence transgresses the borders of time and place. The intrinsic part of us, which passes on, asks of Self, 'Where do you go and where do you come from?' Work done in the area of pre-birth and past-life regressions has added substance and support to this idea.

What has surfaced in return-from-death evidence shows that this same fragment of our being is capable of carrying on where the other part leaves off. Thus we cannot help but look for the contribution of the non-physical existence to physical functioning.

These writings are not meant to make a believer out of the non-believer. That in itself contradicts the idea that people are the maker of their own destiny and act accordingly. It also accepts the principle that it is not in everyone's interest or range to deal with the specific possibilities that are within each of us. No one does, no one would want to, no one could. However an acceptance of reincarnation and the presence of a transitory soul in each person is a basic premise of this material.

If life consists of only one edition,
We should have been able to cancel our subscription.

Belief in reincarnation does have implications. The basic tenet of reincarnation is that the soul is indestructible. If true, what automatically follows is an examination of the reasons we are here on Earth. If there is no reason for self and soulful growth, then why reincarnate? Reincarnation suggests there is purpose to this recycling of lives, not to return once again as a tadpole but to continue in our growth as a spiritual person. Perhaps this is totally philosophical; if so, we must say we both subscribe to this philosophy because it acknowledges that we are thinking, expanding, spiritual human beings.

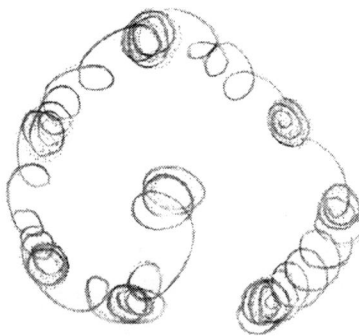

And life goes on

The thought that reincarnation can be dismissed as a figment of imagination is unacceptable within the framework of the soul as a transitory vehicle. Acceptance of creation by holism cannot omit this significant thread, which weaves through the essence of our civilizations from their most primitive to their most expanded and intricate form.

The return to Earth, the renewing of our continuing acquaintance, with all its shapes and forms, is so important that without it, no structure to even our present existence would be left. It is incompatible with the concept of the maturing soul that our brief life years on Earth would be what it is all about.

An insignificant struggle to fight a mammoth, or economic woes as another choice, would make such a futile reason for existing. Our lives can be thought of as being like a necklace, a string of beads, a wind on a coil – each one not excessively outstanding but part of a total. Unable to do without this particular bead, this particular coil, the significance of each one is pointed out, but the final totality is what counts. Each individual part is insignificant by its smallness.

Although the denial of reincarnation seems a great mistake, so is overemphasizing a sign of dwelling on details unnecessarily. We would agree that certain incarnations at a certain time and place in our lives can be of more importance than other ones, but that is where it stops.

Living effectively in the present is the aim.

The essence of reincarnation

Reincarnation and our totality

Compare reincarnation with a series of stories told by the Scheherazade of life: all different, some more interesting than others, but all separate. The plots and players and sometimes place can be a common thread, but that is where it stops. The eventual significance is its totality, the structure of the total, the fibre tying it together. Here we get to the essence of reincarnation, which is the realization that the end total is the ultimate importance of it.

It is when the obvious deviations start coming in, where past lives with their worries and misalignments start interfering with the next stage, that we should give it added attention. Where good should be allowed to permeate and be built upon, so is bad the part that has to be abstained from.

When the goal we set ourselves in between the beads is not dealt with, no progression is possible. A balanced, worked-out life plan is a workable situation that is not always obtained by everyone. It is then that the hard lessons of life are repeated ad nauseam in the physical dimension, with the hurt inflicted to oneself and others in the process.

This is where a compassionate understanding on the part of the therapist is a gift given to help work out these unfortunate circumstances. A small tightrope to be walked yin and yang, where lots of good can be bad and lots of bad can be good.

Reincarnation as fact is a central premise of this material. Though accepted unquestionably as a part of life, the question of avoiding drama is a big one. The beat goes on, but is the role of reincarnation a lead or a bit part? The metaphor of beads and coil is one commonly used in Eastern mysticism, referring to the in-between. This is understood to be the time between physical incarnations when the parameters of the next incarnation are set. If the aim of reincarnation is one of growth towards greater consciousness, then the time spent in the in-between is where the planning is done for re-entry into the physical. It is a time of review and reflection, where our spiritual strategic plan is worked out. There are a number of variables at play here as we assess what we have done and decide what we will do next. If a lifetime is a time of learning, then what we are doing is reviewing lessons learned from our most recent life. Karma, the good and bad debts we carry forward, are both our bonus points and demerits.

What we bring forward

The issue of reincarnation forces us to think with regard to our purpose on Earth and the elements of goal setting. The dilemmas we repeatedly find ourselves in seem so often to take on a similar form.

If the soul were to choose a lifetime of searching for inner perfection, we might find a clue within the repetitive stumbling blocks we encounter. In finding our weak areas, we find our work to be done in the present lifetime.

Again we are reminded to live fully in the present and not to minimize the need for joy, to emphasize the positive, and to support our fellowman.

Reincarnation and our destiny

Consideration that our present life was started and planned in a previous existence does present an interesting dimension. How far back this planning has gone and how much previous learning and conditioning has influenced this present life has to be seriously considered.

Every entity has a vague idea of the effort that has to be put into this life: a more or less developed sense of approaching his or her destiny. A feeling that there is more to this life prompts a goal-setting orientation, which influences decisions being made.

Encouraged or forced by talents and interests, the soul has to choose a path which forces goal setting and self-fulfilment. Personality traits, body rhythms, and inclinations determine how the person is moulded, thus affecting the shaping of his or her environment Self-examination and acceptance of the specific personality tooling, which has been prompted by the soul, hones one towards a deliberate focusing of the specific life one is given or might have chosen.

Birth

Birth is an aspect, a duality, a form that is the vehicle impregnated with that aspect of the God dimension in form – it is tantamount to physical construct.

In the soul dimension, it is a way of grounding a soul to a space in which it can find relevance. To have both functions combined is an everyday occurrence.

The miracle does not stop. We amaze at its wonder daily. The vitalization of spirit consciousness into the physical remains a marvel.

The reason for incarnating at a high level of functionality is tied into many reasons and needs that have to be met. Needless to say, on soul level growth is not necessarily tied into flesh.

The soul could choose to live one of its aspects through unconventional flights and throughways, fares, vehicles, conjunctive experiences, walk-ins, takeovers, and observations. This deals with the abstract dimension. When interacting with the body–mind–spirit, we deal with the physical aspects through our own lives.

Acceptance of reincarnation gives credence to the continuity of soul life and begs us to look at the dichotomy of the many manifestations we express. Given that each soul has its own purposefulness and direction, we can notice the same themes recurring from life to life, including our present existence.

One example that demonstrates this continuity is our friend Devorah, who told us about the research she was doing on Rembrandt's painting *Batsheba*. Many art historians take it at face value, assume the woman is simply taking a bath. Devorah, a Jewish woman in this life, realized that it was not just a bath Batheva was preparing for but a mikvah, a bath used for purification by observant Jews. Devorah saw the mikvah as she gazed at Rembrandt's creation in the Louvre in Paris. Such a bath was required in those days if the king summoned a subject. What Devorah also discovered was that in the painting, Batsheba had three commandments in her hand, one of which was, 'Thou shalt not commit adultery'. She also had David's letter, which was commanding her to do just that. On the letter was a drop of blood. These findings were previously not known, yet Devorah knew them to be true. And when she visited Amsterdam for the first time, she discovered that she knew her way around the Jewish Quarter. It was clear to her that she had been there in the 1600s, when Rembrandt was alive and painting. Today Devorah lives in Canada, is an artist herself, and presently teaches at her local art gallery.

The feeling that there is more to life than day-to-day events and the restlessness such thinking might bring is often an indication of the vague idea of personal destiny. Equal importance is given to the acknowledgement of the impact of reincarnation on present existence – as is the caution not to dwell on it. Living fully in the present is of utmost importance. The previous writing, 'Birth', reminds us that there could be many different reasons for choosing whether to incarnate into physical form. Walk-in does not refer to an off-the-street drop by; rather, it describes beings from the spirit dimension (disincarnate souls) who agree to incarnate into physical form and assume the unfinished business of the person taking leave. The act of walking back into a body may also give them an opportunity to work on their own incompletions.

For more information on the aberrations of reincarnation's natural flows, we recommend Ruth Montgomery's *Strangers Among Us.*

The Longing of the Soul

Living is learning.
Memory is yearning
for times that have gone by.
The essence of creating,
a space in which the 'I'
has found its point of recognition,
a wanting to express
the love of being in a place once known,
a space well blessed.

Exercise: déjà vu

Have you ever had the feeling that this place is not so new?
Have you ever known just where to turn to see the perfect view?
And then you think, 'What am I doing?
I've never been to France'.

Without judgement or thought, recall a time when you felt you experienced a déjà vu. What did you know? Where had you been? Have you ever thought to ask your child if he felt he had lived somewhere else before? The recall of our past existences is usually available before the age of four.

Reincarnation: use in treatment

Holistic treatment includes the concept of reincarnation and strives to integrate body, mind. and soul into the various aspects of our reality: our work, our relationships, and our everyday life. A good example happened when Gerbrig was present at the regression of a gentleman in his early thirties. The therapist asked him to look down at this feet to see what kind of shoes he was wearing, and to his surprise he found he had on a pair of shiny boots. When she directed him to look into a mirror for a full body scan, he saw himself dressed in a Nazi uniform. He was shocked and began to shake because in this life he had deliberately chosen a path of non-violence. In order to make full use of former lives in our interactions with clients, associates, or friends, it is necessary to be aware of this pattern of continuum on a purely non-physical level.

Bridging the old and new medicines

With the changing integration of meditative input into our daily lives, the overt acceptance of altered states has widened our daily belief system. An increasingly flexible attitude, as well as broader levels of interest in a large segment of our population, has resulted in the integration and emergence of a variety of holistic approaches. The mind becomes familiar with meditative techniques and self-sourcing, and it learns to deal with knowledge derived on the subconscious level. This exhilarates the person and opens him or her to the potential of working with the self on a non-physical level. Having omitted the physical, based on a life-cycle system, the question remains what other potential could be available?

The introduction of the parapsychological field into a standard behavioural system needs the reinforcement of a believable scientific approach in order to be able to be integrated as a workable system. That research has been done or is being done in many areas. The deeper understanding of the root of unconscious functioning onto the psychological know-how broadens one's scope greatly.

Recall

Observing the reflex responses of infants heralds a new dimension to this theory of past memory. The latent remnants of reflexes unnecessary to its present-day functioning are still visible. The turning of the head when touched means turning to a food source. A baby's sudden grasping when startled perhaps shows its desire to hold on to the mom's fur in case of danger.

These are all responses to stimuli that far predate memory; they may be based on a genetic memory.

Does one wonder about stimuli less obvious, which are responded to later in life? A whole new field lies open to explore. Many questions show up. Not all stimuli, as Pavlov shows, are genetically based or carried over. Most are nerve responses triggered by an autonomic reaction. In the reincarnation theory, we go out from the assumption that the soul is a transitory vehicle and the mind is a vibrational leveller. In this case, an unconditioned stimulus carried from a time predating the present just needs another stimulus to have a response.

As with all principles derived from the deeper level, it seems wiser not to introduce the subject of reincarnation until a person has developed the ability to sustain an established meditative state and has started to question that there is more to life than this present existence. However, as soon as they feel a sense of trust in the therapeutic relationship, many people will confide that they feel like they have been here before. Asking what this feeling means to the person is the next step. Often what is reported as past experience has relevance to the current growth work of this life.

It was a bit of a shock to Gerbrig and me when we discovered she had been a rather demanding matriarch in Nepal, and I was her daughter-in-law. Everyone waited on her, in that lifetime, and I saw myself continually bringing her food in large wooden bowls. Recall of this lifetime came to both of us at different times. As in the regression mentioned above, looking at her shoes, Gerbrig found they were elaborate felt boots, and without having discussed this, Shelly had bought this very style of boot at a local store that brought them in from Nepal. Both of us find we have a great affinity for Nepalese artefacts and are definitely drawn to handcrafted wooden bowls and primitive woodwork. Even as we write this anecdote, Shelly is wearing a Nepalese shell embellished with silver and turquoise. The metaphors held within our past life memories often bring inner struggles to the fore. Having seen that few people cared when she died in that particular life, today Gerbrig often finds herself in a serving mode. Though these recalls are subjective, they do address a person on a deep level. Both of us have been moved to explore historic and social events in Nepal, and we find that artefacts in museums often feel well-known to us. Despite our

Jewish backgrounds, much of our inspirational reading has a Buddhist slant. These responses can occur without conscious knowledge. From this point on, treatment can go in a myriad of directions.

Storytelling

In this area of past-life memory, a cautionary note has to be emphasized. The recall issue naturally involves both a voluntary and an involuntary aspect. Recall in the verbal sense could easily be overtaken in storytelling. It is so easy to be sucked into a world of imagery, which could so well cloud the real issues.

Honesty on soul level does not deal in terms of anger and revenge. It rather focuses inside on unconditional acceptance and love. Descriptive details about an event in time are describing that specific footstep in the sand, long gone. Inner growth lies in a place far beyond this.

Over the years we were both called upon in our practices to work with past-life regressions. Sometimes the regressions happened spontaneously on the trager table; other times individuals would come to Gerbrig or me individually and ask to be regressed. Always the essential reason for doing this was that something in a past life was bleeding into this life, raising questions and sometimes causing disruptions on the physical or emotional level of the person. A therapist helping someone with recurrent memories gives credence to those memories and helps their clients to link their past lives to relevant themes in this life, such as the woman who kept seeing herself as a nun. Her therapist helped her to link her resistance to becoming pregnant in this life to her former celibate existence.

In working with the soul aspect, it should be clearly kept in mind that present everyday problems can revive forceful karmic memories if current circumstances are sufficiently alike. This can be an indication of either a decision for further growth along similar thematic lines, or attempted resolution of a truly unresolved situation. It can also be a neatly dramatic way to avoid confronting the present, as suggested by the advice given by the team: *The mind as a translator facilitates dealings but can also fool the issues.*

Avoidance behaviour can be a sensible choice on the part of an individual when issues are too overwhelming to handle at a particular time. On the other hand, there can be a temptation to use past lives as a reason or scapegoat for present difficulties. Having an awareness of the deeper themes our souls are addressing is helpful. Then, if the person is insistent that past life is where to work, an approach which allows for a potential tie-in between past-life material and present-day challenges covers all the angles and avoids the possibility of misjudgement on the part of the therapist. Building on Gerbrig's learning from her Nepalese life, a supportive therapist would see her compulsion to assist others as a positive expression of a negative experience and substantiate it as a lesson learned.

Once again, the familiar cautionary note is sounded for everyone involved in a therapeutic setting, both therapist and client alike. Both a careful evaluation and an assessment for every step of the treatment are required. An assessment that includes the weight and validity given to recall of past-life episodes is necessary. This writing reminds us that if we are caught in the dynamic of storytelling, we are still working on the surface level. However, by incorporating all levels of functioning, an understanding that we all approach things from different angles and that creation is multifold must be brought to the therapeutic situation. Such thinking brings an extra dimension to the metaphor sometimes used by our spiritual teaching team, which refers to our multifaceted selves as diamonds or crystals.

Understanding and acceptance of reincarnation does create a tolerance towards others.

Native Elder

'My Earth suit is red', he said.
'It's the one I put on for this journey'.
'Do not pay attention to the colour', he warned.
'It's my soul suit that is important;
its colour is invisible'.

Chapter 7
Karma

For better or for worse

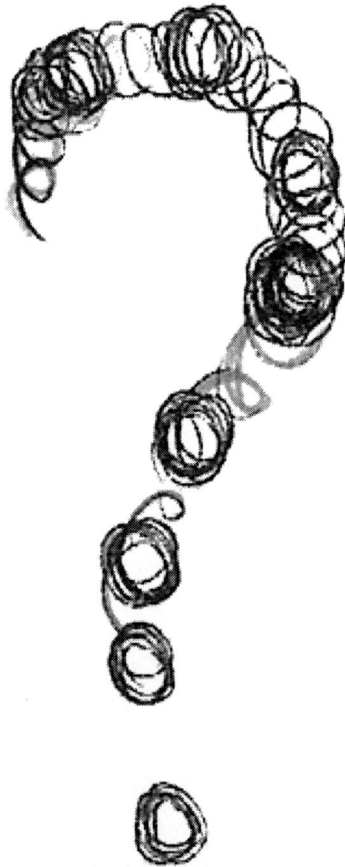

In rough terms, karma implies that whatever we do will come back to us. The word itself stems from Hindu and Buddhist teachings. Karma is a philosophy in Hinduism; Buddhism sees actions as bringing upon oneself inevitable results, good or bad either in this life or in a reincarnation. Karma is the working out of whatever learning the soul has not yet accomplished in its path towards creativity and love *(Random House Dictionary)*.

If time is seen as a simultaneous continuum, we could say that karma could also affect our future lives. Undoubtedly it affected our lives, as for the two of us it was clear from the beginning that we had a karmic contract to meet and study with one another. This realization gave weight to many of our decisions, including the writing of this book.

As we reviewed the writings, we came to realize that karma is a natural continuation of the reincarnation concept; the two cannot be separated. If there is a case for reincarnation, karma is what gives it its essence. Reincarnation acknowledges multiple existences, and karma represents the unfinished work that we bring with us from life to life. The drawing in the last chapter sees our lives on Earth as a necklace. The beads on the necklace represent our individual lives, and the spaces in between represent the periods within which our next lives are planned. This necklace morphs into a question mark in this chapter and represents karma. The question mark has to do with the tasks we will complete as we work off our karma. It begs the question who will we meet, what will our particular talents and interests be, and how will they play out? Understanding the drawings was not always easy; the team used them to tweak our interest of how these pictures highlighted the concepts they taught us. Somehow we always found this exercise to be fun.

The forthcoming reading 'Karma in relation to the evolutionary process of soul' (see p. 73) conveys the message that the there is a purpose behind our existence and that our lives are the arenas for our learning. It is daunting to know that no one but ourselves is honing us. This knowledge encourages us to live life with deliberateness.

Concepts of karma

Karma is whatever you are not, integrating past, projecting future, hanging in between, and dealing with the present in its most realistic aspect. Karma is a philosophy found in many mystic traditions. It indicates that nothing is accidental; Dick or Jane, we don't escape. Life is seen both as a learning and a coping situation.

As souls, we drift in and out of various circumstances, the soul functioning as the instigator and the body as the vehicle. Our life as it is presented is the road we take. In accepting karma we have a powerful tool for uncovering and integrating the purpose we have chosen in this lifetime to enable growth and learning at the level of soul.

Unanswered situations, challenges, and questions will have to be answered at some time. We are the ones in search of answers, and we want to be answered.

Injecting meaning into life

When karma raises its head in the reincarnation debate, one has to resolve this with regard to one's own belief system. As in all issues regarding religion and belief systems, it does not answer to scientific reasoning.

One either accepts it through personal conviction or does not. But if one does, the focus of one's living changes. If one does not, what triggers a person's tendency to go into a personal acquisition mode, either materially or intellectually? Humans would then only align themselves with the other growing things in this world – without much purpose.

Reincarnation does bring this purposefulness into one's existence. One has to live with and accept the consequence of everyday behaviour, whatever form this takes. Its discipline forces a person to accept himself or herself as part of a larger source. It gives meaning to one's living which otherwise would be denied.

It also gives a purpose to religion. Who are we praying to as being God: a stern father, a loving goddess, or Gaia? What is the source of moral behaviour? Why do we call karma our own stern taskmaster?

This writing strongly states that we cannot feel a connection to all living things without believing in former existences. We are further challenged to query, 'To whom are you praying and why?' This gives much to think about regarding purposefulness and a great opportunity to dip into one's own pools of belief and understanding. The conclusion is that the writing points to three things that belief in karma brings: purposefulness, living with consequences, and discipline and a meaning for our existence.

Why karma?

Karma involves many aspects and functions on many levels, from the world to nations to individuals. We can allude once again to the peace-loving gentleman who chose this lifetime as one contradictory to the one he had lived formerly, as a soldier. Karma implies cause and effect as well as planned growth in a specific life.

Karma is the working out of whatever learning the soul has not yet accomplished in its path towards creativity and love. Goals are set in your in-between time when you transcend the dimension of time.

Repetitive challenges in life experiences are often uncovered in repetition of similar behaviours in situations that are, with their slight variations, still so similar. The soul will set up a situation in which the understanding can be acquired, and then the previous mistakes are not repeated. Acceptance of karma in this mode will greatly enhance the soul's ability to grow.

On the other hand, blaming the 'other', projecting causality outward from the self, will cause a lack of resolution and, therefore, a repetition ad nauseam of the essence of the situational dynamics.

Good karma is using what you have. Just living is not using your potentiality.

Impatience is the quality that tends to surface when karma is not used beyond reshaping and redressing the issue. Such impatience on a soul level can be used as a forceful fact-finding of character and choice level – power trips, short fallings, misdemeanours, and so on.

The scale of hurt to self and others can be examined on a deeper level in order to find resolution and eliminate reasons to repeat them. Inner growth will result when the need for ego presenting can be dropped and different relations with our surroundings can be internalized.

In our continuum, everything is only an event. Only the soul is immortal.

Using the larger perspective offered by karma invites us to look at recurring problems and challenges differently. This can defuse highly charged situations and give us creative ways for avoiding or finding solutions to problems, thus releasing us from repetitive behaviour that no longer serves us. Inner growth requires maturity, a state within which one does not have to rely on ego-based behaviour and power struggles.

Relationships will allow others equal space, which in turn will provide a different, more harmonious relationship with our surroundings.

Exercise: flagging our repetitive patterns

Equip yourself with a pencil and paper. Take a few moments to enter into a quiet, detached state. You can do this through noticing your breathing pattern or repeating the progressive relaxation; the point is to detach yourself from the preoccupations of your mind. Make of list of recurring disruptive situations with which you are immediately involved. 'Why am I so deathly afraid of water?' 'Why do I always have a hard time with that person?' Single out the one that holds the greatest charge. Now close your eyes and bring this situation into focus and actually relive the situation, noticing where the annoyance or discomfort resides in your body. Stay with that felt sense and see if it has shape or colour, feeling or emotion. Stay with the feeling until something concrete arises. Perhaps a word will present that defines the sensation. Perhaps there will be a physical shift in your body. Then be your own impresario, rewrite the scene in your own mind, and bring the altered script forward. Notice the feeling when the new is introduced: has anything shifted? Give yourself the opportunity and time to register and hold onto this new feeling.

Footprints

We are aware of dilemmas you might have. They eventually disappear into nowhere, to be replaced by other ones. Only the sand remains, shifting through the millennia, to be formed and shaped only by the creator.

Having a purpose is the only criterion left. Gone is the day-to-day dimension, like a breeze leaving a memory which has no space, just a note of what was.

Increase the feelings and memories that leave a trace of good, and then the slate does not need the bad wiped out. Our work is just that: replacing the good; depleting the bad.

When we focused on the whole issue of karma, our questions seemed endless. We directed these unresolved issues to our spiritual teaching team, referred to in the writing as 'we' and 'our'. They are our connection to a larger dimension, and it is their task to connect us to our spiritual or transpersonal purpose. We believe everyone has the ability to access the larger through his or her own team. To include such an approach into personal growth work makes it less burdensome, because we begin to see that although each of us must do our individual developmental work, we are not alone. As mentioned in former writings and explanations in chapter two, many approaches can be used to access this larger dimension. For some this is accomplished through prayer, for others meditation, and for still others a positive focus.

Karma in relation to the evolutionary process of the soul

The soul aspect within us is the thread holding its lives together; as the perpetuating essence within us, it is the carryover from one existence to the other. Every soul expression is founded within the core of its experiences and failures or victories: retributions of past events. On the road to development and learning, certain attitudes and conditions will advance growth.

Conjugated experiences can enrich or impoverish soul expression. The goal is learning and growth.

Clearing the mind and raising awareness relinquishes the need for reincarnation. This leaves out physical processing as an option of growth – the learning of a language without the travel.

External peace within the physical realm will greatly reduce interference with growth on a soul level. When turmoil is ended and calm achieved, the soul is ready to deal with the next item of growth. Equilibrium within physical functioning is moving on.

Resistance is a path that is diverted, crossed, and turned.

Acceptance of karma mode will greatly enhance the soul's ability to grow.

We will wander past the often ignored signs of destiny. It is part of the struggle of the whole set-up of the soul's growth journey. To be, in essence, is to conquer the diversions and tie in with the ultimate goal of soul life integrated into the everyday.

With acceptance of the concept of the reincarnation of the soul as a reminiscing and transitory vehicle, the question arises as to the effects of the various lives and the learning therein. We acknowledge that time is not the linear dimension we have chosen to experience in the physical realm, but rather it includes a series of existences with specific purposes. Sometimes, however, there is a struggle to stay on our chosen path; we can become diverted and postpone our opportunities for growth.

Our goal over the years as we worked with this material was to do the very things we are now prescribing. We set aside specific times regularly when we cleared a time, quieted our minds, and practiced the exercises we listed in the chapters over and over again. The benefit of this practice raised our awareness and kept us on our spiritual track. Was it easy? Not always!

Wrong choices – a need to withdraw

We wrestled with presenting such emotionally laden topics as crib death and other early withdrawals from a life. Yet we could not overlook the beauty of the material given us, nor could we avoid including material answering some of the hardest questions. As always, we were moved by the expansive and non-judgemental nature of the thoughts contained in the writings.

A new start to the old problem, when gross mistakes are made in choosing the future, might prompt one to contemplate withdrawal. The mysterious crib death is a great way out, but so are many other means available, and they are often utilized. In the 'we are we' concept, mistakes are also made in the in-between. When done, the entity might withdraw and can do so without incurring negative karma. When still in the human infant cycle (this is meant in earthly terms and is not meant in terms of soul cycles), if one is not able to withdraw, the best has to be made of a life process started with wrong indications involved. There are two possible explanations for withdrawal:

  – Consciously chosen and used as life experience
  – A thrown-upon (as in not having been chosen) and miscalculated life; this second choice could carry an attitude of obvious disdain for life

Yin and yang: making the best of a bad choice

The goal now is to make a positive experience out of a negative start. If and when negativity is not overcome, we deal with a maladjusted personality. This person not only has to learn the same lesson again but also incurs so much negative karma that sets one back in soul growth. This is a drastic drama which should be avoided. A distinction has to be made between:
  – A wrong lifetime choice
  – A natural occurrence
  – A diversion on our regular path

Anecdotal writing: early withdrawal – a personal account by a sixty-year-old woman

I was invited to sit in circle with a group who had brought a deep-trance medium to their gathering. The following is a personal account by a sixty-year-old woman.

The light was turned out, and I sat waiting for things to happen. Voices seemed to take turns having their say in matters that seemed rather trivial to me. I wondered why people were called from the great beyond to engage in this 'over the backyard fence' conversation. After some time, I wondered how long this was going to last. The people seemed to know what they were doing, and I settled into some kind of state of resignation.

Suddenly I saw a light area appear in front of me; it slowly took shape. My youngest sister came into focus – the way a picture would when it is being developed. She smiled at me and flicked her hair the way she used to. I recognized her clothing. She had died accidentally, many years before, at the age of sixteen. I was mesmerized. 'Well', she said, 'do you like this? Isn't this great?' I realized I should utilize the moment. I told her I had just been home and that I still missed her. I added that I had been wondering how it would have been if she had still been with us, together with her husband and children. She raised her eyebrows and, looking surprised, said, 'I was not supposed to live any longer; there never was going to be a husband …' I thanked her for giving me this lesson and apologized for not having lived within my own belief system, one that includes the continuity of life. She smiled and then slowly disappeared.

This moment changed my life! I had been taught a lesson that had come from outside my personal earthly dimension. In that moment, I understood that soul has its own path, and a life can be complete within its own time span, however short or long that might be. I honoured the memory of my sister by giving my daughter her name.

Thirty years later, my first grandson was born. We received him with all the love we had and watched him develop and grow. When he was a year old, his distinct personality began to emerge, and his features took definite form. We quickly noticed that his physical resemblance, behavioural traits, and interests mirrored those of my late sister. A photograph proved what we all had suspected – it was like looking into my sister's eyes …

Events like these often seem to appear when least expected, jolting us out of a place of complacency. But our belief system, which aligns with life's continuity, helps us to reconcile ourselves with these situations. They remind us that we do live our lives on many dimensions.

The writings allude to the existence and inevitability of karma and its mysterious ways. Good or bad, we will be confronted by our deeds over the course of many lives. The situations that we attract will also include an element of choice in how we select to work things out. This is the process of self-search and self-examination. We are encouraged to stretch ourselves, using the tool of self-evaluation to question standard belief systems, our own, and those of the society around us. This approach to the concept of karma asks us to accept responsibility for our actions and to go inward to find answers rather than projecting blame onto others. Such an attitude, though it may appear to be hard, can in fact be very empowering, shifting us from the passive role of victim into a proactive role. This puts a very different slant on the hardships that life presents. The dialogue continues.

Hardship is as deep as needed and as hard as allowed.

Soul mates

The next writings dare to address such sacred cows as soul mates. Without going into great detail, several anecdotal writings furnish us with the good and bad of soul mates reuniting. So often seen as positive, they offer a polar point of view for consideration. Even the highly sought-after soul mate can bring his or her own karmic points of reckoning. However, when all is said and done, it is all just learning. Many books have been written on the topic of soul mates. Richard Bach and Thomas Moore are two authors who have addressed this subject.

Soul mates, often so highly exalted, can also be the ones driving negative impact within our lifetime. All is learning.

In *Soulmate* Richard Bach portrays the positive side of soul mates.

A soulmate is someone who has locks that fit our keys, and keys to fit our locks. When we feel safe enough to open the locks, our truest selves step out and we can be completely and honestly who we are; we can be loved for who we are and not for who we're pretending to be. Each unveils the best part of the other. No matter what else goes wrong around us, with that one person we're safe in our own paradise. Our soulmate is someone who shares our deepest longings, our sense of direction. When we're two balloons, and together our direction is up, chances are we've found the right person. Our soulmate is the one who makes life come to life.

In *The Bridge Across Forever*, Bach explores the meaning of fate and soul mates in this modern-day fairy tale based on his real-life relationship with actor Leslie Parrish. It tells the story of a knight who was dying and of the princess who saved his life. Bach writes in his opening greeting, 'It's a story about beauty and beasts and spells and fortresses, about death-powers that seem and life-powers that are'. On the earthly plane this is about the riveting love affair between two fully human people who are willing to explore time travel and other dimensions together while grappling with the earthly struggles of intimacy, commitment, smothering, and whose turn it is to cook. Their love affair and happy ending inspired many enthusiastic fans. Years later, some of these fans were devastated to discover that this match made in heaven didn't manage to stick (the couple is no longer together). But in an interview, Bach explained that lovers don't have to stay married forever to be lifetime soul mates. 'Read this as a lesson about love's enchantments and possibilities, but don't count on this book to keep you and your mate on the bridge across forever'.

Thomas Moore, in his book *Soul Mates: Honoring the Mysteries of Love and Relationship*, describes a soul mate as 'someone to whom we feel profoundly connected, as though the communication and communing that take place between us were not the product of intentional efforts, but rather a divine grace. This kind of relationship is so important to the soul that many have said there is nothing more precious in life'.

Treasured

Sprung from different generations,
Living a certain oneness,
A friendship unexplained.
Moments laced with humour and respect,
Infused with each other's energy,
Communication without words.
United on levels not understood,
A relationship centuries old.

In these writings, all is seen as growth and purposefulness in relation to soul. Growth and life in all its forms is presented as the playing field. Life is acknowledged as something to be treasured.

Karma: its applications in personal and therapeutic self-growth situations

The main consideration when using karma with clients or when seeking to make one's own personal changes is to look for patterns of events. We might ask whether we are achieving the outcomes we wish. This enables both individual and therapist to discern the deeper level of the learning process and to avoid focusing too much on details which may obscure the true issue at hand.

However, working with karmatic events can be tricky because subjective tale telling and personal symbols might cloud the events. Some situations might also contain upsetting aspects. Although the issues may imply a specific motive for the soul to be undergoing, those that appear could be challenging for both therapist and client. The goal of improved relationships and conditions has to be kept firmly in focus. This, in conjunction with supportive understanding, should enable the client to find a workable solution. Regardless of karmatic overtones in the therapeutic setting, we should emphasize and encourage the living of life in the present.

Nowhere in therapeutic situations should there be an attitude of blame. A therapist can help a client alleviate feelings of guilt and, going further, can bolster the client. For instance, rather than chastising a person who is overweight, the therapist can help her recognize and accept herself. This can be a significant part of the healing process. Once the weight gain or major injury is seen as a learning process in this life, and perhaps even linked to an emotional or abusive cause, it can then be used as a means for moving on and into productivity. Accept and loving who and what we can be is groundwork for developing a plan for change. As therapists we must remember that we are never privy to the chosen path of an individual's soul.

The question can be asked, 'What am I trying to teach myself by experiencing this event, pain, trauma, or joy?' Such questioning can produce a deep and heartfelt sigh and a feeling that life is worth living indeed.

Dimensions of karma

Karma, on the level of personal choice, is a philosophy which can be taken or left as the reader wishes. If left, the skills needed to resolve day-to-day situations will remain the same. The missing aspect will be the conscious understanding of the implications for the soul.

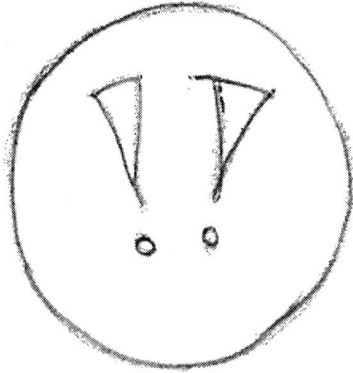

Karma: a two-edged sword

Karma has two aspects. One is our awareness of it on a day-to-day level; this deals with both behavioural patterns and solutions that dissolve misunderstanding. There is a second and higher aim of karma which has a deeper underlying aspect – that of soul growth. Soul growth, as previously stated, aims to increase spiritual awareness and return one to the source of creation (see the first writing, 'Concept of creation' in 'The maturing soul' section of chapter five). According to the karma philosophy, decreased tension on the personal level is helpful in enabling us to achieve effective fulfilment of the destiny of the soul, tantamount to walking in a state of wakefulness versus sleep walking.

Anecdotal writing: letting go

This is a personal writing about searching for answers for a forty-two-year-old woman who came to us as a client questioning a past-life scenario and having a hard time with the recapitulation of that past memory.

Self-protection with regard to denial is assessing a situation within the good of the denial. Tabula rasa at the source of the thought pattern allows the freedom of a de-automatization process. With acceptance of karma comes the thought frame of pattern development – be it good or bad. Tabula rasa within this framework is the absolution of ingrained pattern information.

Functioning within the framework of the oneself is exploration of a concept within the range of one's functioning. Again, whether there be good or bad findings, it is examining the rooms of one's abode, so to say. Indeed, it is making one's abode an area of work to project oneself from! It is comparable to the house of the snail, the shell of a turtle. It is the last boundary between the real self in here (real Self) and the real self out there, reality out there, and wherever these two may be merging. Emergence of the Self out of the grip of the self and its demands is what we strive for. On the higher soul level, this Self takes in a larger range than that of the day-to-day persona.

The fullest awareness on the highest level is reachable in the benign sphere of the afterlife, when evaluation is desired. It is giving the due respect of living physically in the realm of physical functioning, which is at the mercy of neurological processing.

Clearing of mind and raised awareness relinquish the need for reincarnation. This leaves out physical processing as an option of growth – the learning of a language without the travel.

Within the realm of self-choice we also have the right to self-exploration; do see this as your option. Give yourself the confidence that you are the product of great learning and growth. Having undertaken your area of growth, you are encouraged to grow and replenish through awareness. Accept past-life work as the recall of a growth process, which will slot in easily. Take one step at a time for added growth in this area.

Try to function with one's dream field to use your subconscious not your conscious as a tool. External peace within the physical realm will greatly reduce interference because only when turmoil is ended and calm achieved can the soul be ready to deal with the next. Equilibrium within this functioning is a moving on process. Look at the drawing for meditative purposes. Digging deep is done here from the outside in, not from the inside out. Strive for contentment.

Wow – so much contained within this poetic writing, so many points, and so much instruction! Beginning with a very general tone, we focused quickly on the individual person, offering very specific directions and tools, even taking care to use the individual's own terminology. Its messages, however, are relevant to us all.

'Tabula rasa' comes from the Latin words 'tabula', which means 'slate', and 'rasa', which means 'erased'; it refers to the mind as a clean slate. In the development of a person, it is the child in its uncluttered state, prior to socialization or indoctrination. In this writing, 'wiping the slate clean' is not only tolerated, it is encouraged. There is no need to review endlessly either past material or past lives. Live life in the present, she is advised. Sidestepping is okay; evaluation can occur in the in-between time. Loosen yourself, she is told, from the grip of the everyday events and persona (small self), so that she can expand into the larger dimension of the transpersonal Self.

Give yourself full credit for your abilities – notably, the ability to explore the many rooms you inhabit. Do so in everyday life and utilize the dreamtime to access the subconscious levels – a vast area of resource, the trip without the travel.

This writing is not an easy one. Each sentence is laden with information. Essentially it emphasizes that to find peace within our physical realm, we can retreat into meditation, that place of deep reflection, and infuse our reflection with a specific focus on contentment.

Review, replenish, retreat into meditation,
and above all, seek contentment. Wow!

A soul is a soul is a soul:

soul levels and their age equivalents

Soul levels and their ages have found their way into the vocabulary through the description of the human soul. In order to be able to describe abstract reasoning, help in the form of established equivalents is used in order to rationalize conceptual reasoning.

Humankind, in its search for Self and to explain its larger functioning, has found itself in a situation of having to describe less, little, more, good, better, best, small, medium, and large. On a scale of growth and development, a position is conquered and worked on, which then requires a progressive move, changing dimensionally. The equivalent of young, old, and so forth, soul is the level of understanding from the point of the observer. A soul is a soul is a soul. Growth and learning is an external dimension of that soul.

For therapists, in this matter the soul's level or age is a tool. It is clients' knowing what this means which gives it its use. See soul level as the development of man in its earthly dimensions. See its uses and its limitations. Man and woman as soul is old, whatever it is named. How old is young-old, and how old is old-old? How much is upper-middle, and how much is middle-upper or lower-upper? These terms may benefit someone, but what do they say from a judgemental point of view?

We like to refer to young as being the equivalent of vibrant and energetic, striving for whatever we think a young person strives for. The amorphous term might think of young as impetuous and less seasoned. But young ones can be very deliberate and very wise.

Does 'old' bring automatic wisdom with it? Old age might be the impetuous personified but tempered by loss of energy. The savant, as an example, is like a young soul but is often the old soul who withdrew in many aspects. Use old, young, and all descriptions with wisdom. It is a tool – but it is also a pitfall for handicap. Do use it as one of the assessments in order to fill a framework.

Our particular vantage point gives no gold stars to old or new souls; all are equally important, and we find no relevance in comparison. Soulful growth is a matter of self-awareness and self-development. It matters little where you start. As humans it is hard to think we are on level ground given the beatification of individuals in the church or our deification of sports and movie celebrities. These are earthly notions of hierarchy.

The soul is eternal; it will never be young or old.

Logic revisited

The material as is describes the higher aim of karma. Labelling and hierarchical terms are a very concrete way of expressing ourselves on a physical level. Because life is consciously lived on the physical level, terminology as such has certain merits, although only in explanation. Logic is very superficial; it serves everyday lingo to sort things out. Logic on eternal level is without words. Take care to note the awareness of depth of our existence.

A meditative poem

What Is an Age, What Is a Stage?

An age is a life level;
a stage is a life plateau.
Life is just a fraction of eternity,
a series of breaths with a beginning and an end.
A breath which carries the warning
that it might be the last one,
the chugging of a machine, the emission of gases.
Life and lives are a part of learning –
no beginning, no end.
Some are good,
some are not so good,
and some are awfully bad.

We on this earth are here to help each other.
Each does some, some do nothing,
but we all have this lifeline in common:
lots of breathing, lots of repeating.
All make for learning.

Whee …

Giggles and wiggles,
Spiders and snails,
Puppies and kittens,
Snowballs and pails,
Candy and popcorn,
Ice cream and tea –
I still have the child in me.

Chapter 8
Pets and peeves

From bogged down to simplicity

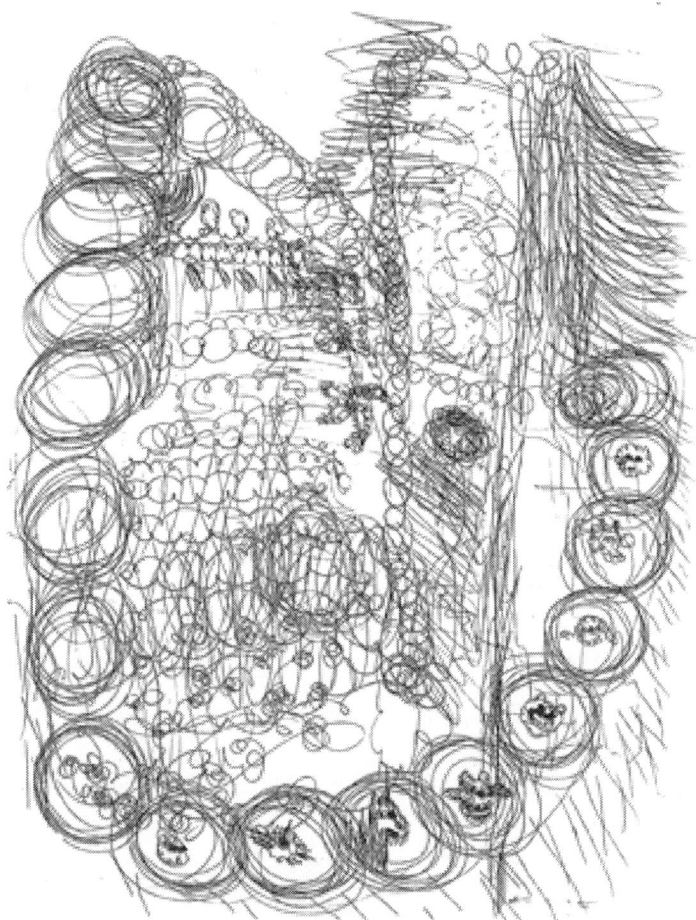

After the heavy tone of the last chapter on karma, we sense a shift. From the get-go, we knew that the material we were studying was different. The automatic drawing, which the team referred to as *Les Petites Choux*, was the clue; it set the stage for a different vein to be tapped. We were forced to look at our theatrical selves and the dance we dance on the stage we call our world. We realized that we were the observer plus the dancer. Despite our retreat into working with this material, it only served to remind us that in our busy lives we also piled up our own pets and peeves as we functioned within our families. Although minimalism sounded like a simple and sane way to live, it proved to be impossible in the Western world. It was an endless struggle to resist taking home the latest snack pack toy or purchasing the newest must-have gadget. As we looked at ourselves, we had a good chuckle, realizing we would have to answer yes to the question posed: is humanity like cabbages, passively watching a stage surrounded by their 'pet appendages'? We had to admit to that humanity, not knowing quite how to step off of the stage. And we must also admit that looking at these controversial sides of ourselves was and remains difficult.

As we studied this drawing further, we found ourselves calling this material les petites choux writings with an element of great fondness. Though not surprised by the power and relevance of this drawing, we were astonished and delighted to find how sequential and relevant the ensuing material was. No accidents! One writing led into the next, deepening and simplifying the information.

As you will see when you read on, like a dog biting its own tail, we were circling back to concepts discussed in the beginning chapters of the book, but this time we took them into the arena of application. Are we picking up the layers of peeled onion skin that have fallen, or are we like the snake, slithering out of what no longer fits as we grow into a new skin that can house our expanded condition?

Do we need to be reminded that life is encumbered?

We were pleasantly surprised when the team shifted emphasis in these writings. They started to discuss the interlopers into our lives, using the phrase 'pets and peeves' to describe all the things that grab our attention and require our energy.

But don't imagine that these pets and peeves are all negative. They are often the very things that pad our lives with comfort and pleasure. Yet again, the team presented us with a changed way we could view our surroundings – sometimes uplifting, sometimes …

Some Kind of Splendour

I dance midst fairy webs,
With visions of magnificence
As I bog in the mundane.

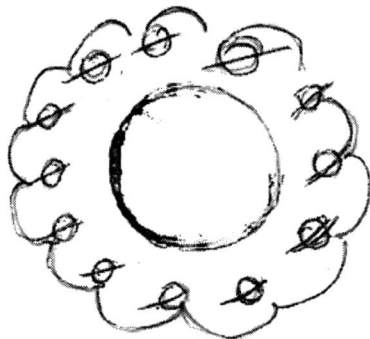

Our surroundings mirror the viability of the integral Self, because the soul has chosen to express itself in this particular life.

The embodiment of our lifetimes' experiences, together with the needs for our present circumstances, are reflected in the forms and uses and abundance of our resources.

Our pets and peeves are reflected in the compassion and control we show in our behaviour, and they emphasize the fact of our humanity and fallibility. Each person will find a unique way to express commonly experienced events.

In fact so intensely unique is each person that it is futile to attempt a comparison with another. In our continuum, everything is just an event; only the soul is immortal.

Simplicity

Simplicity is in perfection. What perfection is in simplicity! One does not exist without the other. Spirituality does not need words and coaching; it is you and you alone. Choices made are choices dealt with. You could let them go.

The need for simplicity forces one to look at all that needs attention around us. Investment, time, and money do not always answer us with a return that is acceptable.

Simplicity is having time to nurture the self in the less depleted state. Simplicity is having time for family and friends. Simplicity is looking for value based on a personal level, not on financial values. Simplicity is making a deliberate choice in a complex world. Simplicity is not 'buying into it'. Simplicity is a show of strength.

Gain one, drop one. Drop one, gain one. Gain is me.

Although impossible to ignore life's tribulations, do know that we talk about fleeting patterns around us. Existing but not really there, the patterns are a movie on a screen, there now and gone again. Take a step back and live your life. Obligation is self-imposed; there is no must. Love is dropping the pets and peeves; love is there but deep inside.

This meditative poem is profound in its simplicity. It invites us inward to assess what we know and what is really important. No must have or must do; just the observation to what is happening in the moment.

Meditative Poem

There is really nothing you must be,
And there is nothing you must do.
There is really nothing you must have,
And there is nothing you must know.
There is really nothing you must become,
However it helps to know that fire burns,
And when it rains, the earth gets wet.

Exercise: uncovering what is essential

Use the exercises already given to relax your body and clear your mind. Have a pencil and notebook handy and then sit comfortably and close your eyes. To begin, allow your mind to take an imaginary meditative walk through your world, the place where you live and function. Notice your physical surroundings and the objects within them. Now ask what things seem to strengthen and empower you, and which feel like they are burdens. Do they require too much care? Do you really need this?

As you are making your assessment, be aware of how much time and energy is required to obtain and care take your possessions. Take note of what you feel and take a moment to write down your discoveries. Then return to your relaxed state and close your eyes. Place yourself back into your living world and imagine you are able to float above your surroundings. From this place of observation, determine what is important to you and gradually rebuild your space. Notice the difference and take note of it as you make your notations. This exercise can be repeated and also applied to your friends, relationships, and work. This knowledge can redefine your interpretations of 'must have' and 'must do'.

A friend related this story to us. When deciding whether or not she needed a lamp, she said to her husband, 'Subtracting time away and sick days, I have calculated that I lifted this lamp twice a week to dust underneath it, that makes one hundred lifts a year. Do we want to add another hundred lifts? That could be two thousand lifts in twenty years'.

Junk we like to surround ourselves with

Junk is the large accumulation of paraphernalia we like to surround ourselves with. The series of props – emotional and material, human and animal – are our protective shield around our essence.

It is very hard to penetrate this forceful projection of self because the protection is very carefully built up. It constitutes a shield comprised of a large variety of non-connecting occurrences and various physical and material forms. It is the face we present to our worldly connections and is so dominant that it can prevent our features from surfacing. They are our masks, so to speak.

The connections between peel and kernel are scant. They are the loose wrappings that are chosen by each of us to protect ourselves. Dismantling completely is cruel and of no importance to the disrober because it is the most superficial presentation of one's front and has to be seen as such. Everyone and everything needs a protective shield, and its shape, form, and size is very often incidental. The insight to the existence of it is very important.

Rank and file fall away; so do possessions and poverty, or beauty and disease. Behind this barrier is where the vibrational level of the entity exists, protecting and surrounding our innermost part of being, the soul or essence. This latter and final part is completely unburdened by physical hindrances and attributions. It is the G-dhead in each of us, the essence of our spirit, the final truth of all love.

Encumbrances

These writings both honour life's tribulations and encourage us not to be too bogged down in them. In fact, this message is quite stern in the writing titled 'Encumbrances', which acknowledges the force of the struggle to balance the drive to meet basic needs with the search for soul/peace. Perhaps the statement 'be in the world but not of it' aptly describes what we are encouraged to strive for. This well-known phrase was coined by the British essayist William Hazlitt. In his essay 'On Living to One's Self', the original quote was, 'What I mean by living to one's self is living in the world, as in it not of it'.

Although there is a great deal of latitude given to personal choice and direction, inherent as well is a plea both for dropping the burdens of earthly constraints and for committing to the growth of the spirit. However, the writings in no way dismiss our earthly existence. Rather, in the writing on earthly foundations, we are reminded to examine what brings real meaning to our lives and to function as enablers to our fellow earthly mates.

Once again, we find the terminology to be very deliberate on the one hand and chewable on the other. Initially the word 'junk' is used to describe our earthly collections of things and obligations, while 'pets and peeves' is the term used in the writings to come. We went back to

our trusty *Random House Dictionary* (2005) for a definition of junk and found the following:
1. old or discarded material objects
2. a seagoing ship used in Chinese waters
3. informally, narcotics

Is it possible for us to drop our pets and peeves, those attachments to earthly concerns? Can they set us adrift far from our intended destination or propel us forward or off course? Can they drug us? What other connections or relevant metaphors can one find?

The concept of soul anchored onto earthly notions – desires and obsessions, good and evil, want and need – are all based on concepts empowering us on the physical level. Balance between the soul's peace and demands for basic needs are an enduring power struggle. It is not for nothing that this fluctuating condition is chosen.

Reincarnation into the physical, the pleasure of growth, and the tribulations of getting there are the means to soul development. Unfortunately, the joy often seems to be missing.

Sometimes the struggle to survive and pad ourselves just seems to be too seriously taken. We encumber ourselves to the point of drowning. Let go of the many so-called physical pleasures – temporary enjoyments with great price tags.

The time to harvest is being able to see the sun shine, the earth move along, and the waters sound. Lots of suffering is caused by home-concocted worries. Drop many of the responsibilities that are not people based. Our personal growth is still based on growth of the Self and its corresponding enabling of our fellow mates.

This writing is very earth based, because no growth and development is achieved when the foundations are in uproar and turmoil. Higher achievements have many concepts – one often excluding the other.

You choose!

Freeing the soul for dummies

Our interactions with the team weren't always so serious. 'Freeing the soul for dummies' was a title we giggled over when told to use it in one of our Thursday morning study sessions. We had to trust that the team was well aware that seekers of all sorts are always looking for simplified solutions to any endeavour. It jolts us out of the ancient and archaic and reminds us of the relevance of this material to today. This writing harkens us back to the introductory chapters of the book on soul, adding a 'how-to' to the material. The process is relatively simple: drop your junk and tune inward.

In order to free the soul, the human has to unburden from each of the pets and peeves in the protective shield. This is dismantling in the truest sense.

The old soul, especially with its awareness of growing urgency, will be the one burning its karma the fastest. Vibrational rate increases fast, and tuning to different levels is a closer possibility. Even in rest, this soul does not function on slower vibrational levels and relates on a psychic level, which attracts other old souls and transcendental souls.

It is when our junk is dispensed that soul existence can develop to the fullest. Infant, baby, and young souls are examining, building, and perpetuating life's appendages, which include disease and power.

The mature soul begins to experience a need to introspect; it will grow in its awareness but will need the usual protection as a reminder. It is the old soul who needs unburdening.

In different lives, we change the wrappings that surround us. We examine our junk, some valuable, some not, but nothing is indispensable. We ourselves stay the same – the soul stays the same, but our vibrational speed changes – lessons learned, levers upward.

The Robes Speak

Patricia's black velvet robe lay on the floor.
I watched her pick it up,
Saw her feel its softness.
Around her it transformed into colourful pieces,
And she was strengthened.
Rosalie's was red with golden threads.
All the court admired the robe,
Knew its strength when she was cloaked.
She let them take it off,
And with it went her power.

My robe was silk and shimmering;
Appliqué enhanced the deep pink
Mandala of hand-painted flowers.
One disapproving look, the colours bled,
And with it my assurance.
I awoke.

Back to square two

Let it be known that life is less of a mystery than what we think! Major decisions and changes are less an external motive than a result of inside growth. What is needed is a move towards a triple processing of body-mind into soul-spirit factor, which is basic to understanding this approach, and which will be discussed later.

Combine the three factors into one, body-mind-spirit, and the chapter is closed!

In this chapter's final drawing, the flower steps off the stage, out from its encumbrances, to take responsibility for its own growth – the integration of body, mind, and spirit.

We are then reminded of the complexity of our being and the interplay of all four of our aspects: body, mind, soul, and spirit. The writing points out that in order to make changes in our life, we must choose to do so, and the process of doing is one of going inward, an ideal transition to our next chapter.

A reminder!

Cells are cells, mind is the changing vibrational level, soul is the reminiscing and transitory vehicle, and spirit soars unfettered by earthly concerns. In different lives, we change the wrappings that surround us — some valuable, some not.

Nothing is indispensable; the soul stays the same.

Portraits in Glass

Stepping back,
Looking into windows,
Reflections …
Images caught between the panes.
Trapped, part of a drama
Until I remember
Windows …
To open or close as I see fit.

Windows to the past,
Memories, shattered or smooth,
Shards …
To help construct the whole.
Windows, wrapped in dreams,
Portals to the future,
Visions …
Reservoirs, watery and undefined.

Chapter 9
To learn is to grow

Until I perceive, I cannot see

Learning, Learning, Learning

All is learning, learning, learning;
some goes fast,
some slow.
You choose.

Every soul expression is founded
within the core of its experiences,
failures and victories alike.

Retributions of past events,
but a lifetime is
a commodity

too precious to waste
by looking constantly over one's shoulder.

As we round the bend towards the final chapters of this book, we are moving even more into application. We are often referring back to earlier material, putting it to use within a context of learning. As the writings shifted in tone and topic, we were required to adjust our way of being. As our spiritual teaching team began to focus on utilizing this information in our everyday lives, they harkened us back to our *Uncharted Corners of Consciousness*. We in turn realized we had to make a transition from merely studying the material to actually incorporating it in to our daily lives.

The writings reminded us that learning and doing have much to do with our mindful connection to a greater beyond. We were provided with a framework within which to examine our relationship with the larger dimensions, while effectively functioning within our everyday world. The drawings also changed from universal in nature to ones of greater specificity. A glance back through the pages will offer you yet another way to appreciate the progression of the book as it takes us deeper into ourselves. The channelled drawings can be used for contemplation.

At the outset of this chapter, you see a drawing that looks like the lens of a camera – a clear representation of focusing or zooming in. This drawing shares many of the same elements seen in the drawing on being all you can in chapter three. The three circles are missing the lines that transform the image into a shutter. Are we being shown that our lens can only have the ability to hone in on a deeper level once we have integrated spirit into our being?

Vessels

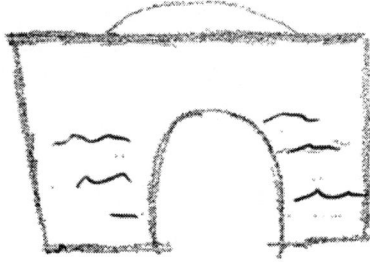

The vessels from which humankind drinks are the vessels of learning. This learning, which is done continuously, is part of our essence. The essence determines and establishes our being; it can represent our functioning bridge or dependency yoke. It is said that the vessel has to be emptied before it can be filled again.

When learning is described as the yoke or bridge, it reminds us of the broader impact learning has on the human: a gateway to another dimension of knowledge, yet a burden to carry. So well emphasized is this yoke and the responsibility knowledge carries with it, that no hiding behind ignorance is allowed.

This alludes to the fact that, through the uncluttering of the self, opportunity is created, allowing a thought to grow. It can expand in this emptiness to create its own form, which can construct itself removed from previous concepts.

In connecting to the pets and peeves idea, we can allow ourselves to realize how clutter and entrapment could so easily thwart clarity. Disconnection from everyday hassle is a must in order to maintain contact with the self on the unfettered level – and to connect to the deeper Self.

The material repeatedly directs us to move with our feet firmly planted on the earth in the physical, everyday world, to take time out to walk, smell the roses, and converse with our fellow beings. It is also acknowledged that in order to connect with our deeper selves, we must withdraw into silence and reflection. The writing reinforces that repetitive practice will enhance one's ability and flexibility to connect with the expanded dimensions.

Uncharted

I seek the familiar,
Walking paths I have walked before,
Stirring between identities.
All is different.
Disconcerted, uncertain, feet unfirmly planted.
Carefully I place one step before the other.

The Dada of doing things

This chapter invites us to break the masts and rip down the sails, to step so deeply into the Self that the unknown is not only accepted but welcomed. Throw away your worship of predictability, they say, and let go of what you know and your need for predicting outcomes. We were being rudely shaken out of our comfort zone, and so it was somewhat reassuring to check the history books and see why our team had used Dadaism as their preferred metaphor. Let's see what they say!

The group used Dadaism as a metaphor in this writing. William S. Rubin, in his book *Dada and the Surrealist Art*, describes Dadaism as 'the style of a group of artists, writers, musicians and filmmakers of the early twentieth century who exploited accidental and incongruous effects in their works'. We refer to this as 'random acts of creativity'. The movement itself was birthed in Zurich in 1916. With the advent of the First World War, the Dadaists, refugees themselves, became disillusioned with the state of the world and felt that the conditions of the times signalled the end of the world of art. In fact, they saw no reason for art in its current state to exist in the world. They chose to mock conditions by randomly choosing the French term for a child's hobbyhorse, 'dada', as the label for their art form. It was a movement born of despondency. As stated by the German poet, Catholic mystic, and pacifist Hugo Ball in a diary entry made June 18, 1916, 'The Dadaist is fighting against the agony of the times and against the inebriation with death' (Rubin, 1985).

Dadaism is an apt metaphor for this material, which stresses the individual nature of how people express themselves. It insists that accommodation for these unique traits should be made. It advocates for the severance of our attachment to the physical world and its encumbrances in exchange for our reattachment to the contemplative realms.

Much of what this writing is about is shown in the drawing below. The bottom circle, humankind in our earthly form, is being stretched beyond itself into another form represented by the top circle. Yet the two exist simultaneously: as we advance into this learning stage, we should pay attention to the signs, enter into silence, and let the clutter of life (our pets and peeves) slip away. While doing so, we learn to walk with our feet astride both dimensions. When we look at the Dada drawing in this chapter, it supports the message of the writing to find creative expression amidst chaos. We found that the coil shapes of Dada were also present when we were forced to look at reincarnation and karma. The spiral of the beat in its openness is in sharp contrast with the question mark of karma's spiral. Are we being prodded to look at the drawings more intently as instruments of learning and understanding? Yes, they invite us into a more active exploration of the Self. The compactness and airiness of the spirals also differ.

What does this have to do with Dadaism? The following writing chooses to confront our sensibilities by juxtaposing these two seemingly unrelated approaches, Dada and the contemplative life. There are similarities to both movements. Both require a deliberate and definite focus; both ask us to leave the comfort of our known parameters and step into areas less charted. From despair, Dadaists were able to create a new and viable art form. The same possibilities are available to those who walk the path of contemplation: 'Deliberate acts of deconstruction for purposes of reconstruction' (Rubin, 1985). Here the outcomes can be random. The challenge is to venture into unknown realms knowing the disruption and chaos that will almost certainly occur.

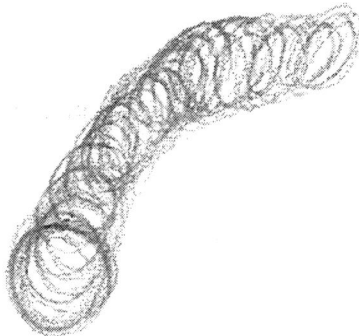

Be aware, pay attention, heed the signs. When we go into the learning phase, we have to realize that this is done in silence and in quietness of mind – uncluttered with issues which are basically irrelevant and disturbing.

On the soul level we like to see ourselves as both whole and complete in order to move on our spiritual travel. Especially on the level of increased awareness and contemplation, we like to think of ourselves as the more complete notion of what the soul should be; an example of increased awareness with diminished 'gravitudinal' burdens, so named for earthly notions which pull us such as possessions, enhancements, and so forth.

What is important on the earth level does not even exist on the contemplative one. We like to endow ourselves with the ability to stand with one foot in one dimension and the mind or higher level in another dimension. We need to stretch the self. We do want to drop the pets and peeves.

We emphasize the need for joy of self-expression without the fear of new ways of seeing the world around. With a sense of adventure and the tossing away of preconceived notions, we can then step into arenas previously unknown or avoided. Only then can we see behind the horizon. This shows the sense of confidence in one's self, one that requires excessive courage and strength. And that is what we call the 'Dada of doing things'.

We must be willing to deconstruct in order to reconstruct.

Both of the following writings illustrate the 'Dada of doing things' – a distinct imprint of the person the writing is about offered in text and pictures. Each shows a different end of the spectrum concerning self.

A thirst for knowledge,
A thirst for knowing.
The love of being here,
An endless growing.

Think of a thorough and respected individual who has 'nothing matters'
and 'let be' in her demeanour, who possesses a forgiving attitude, growing
capacities, and a love for her fellow man. Her work is a reflection of herself.
The intensity of wanting to be and a dedication to her principles has enabled
her to focus herself to within a situation, which is merely a stepping-stone.
With the abilities to overcome problems as they arise, her place is one of
satisfaction in the achievement of living and presenting her deeper Self.

Growth of self, as measured in the I, is having achieved a level which is
workable under any condition.

The love of being,
The care of giving,
The want for knowing
Whatever is there.
The feel of finding
And passing along
Is knowing that the self

Has cared about being,
But is forever going
To a point beyond.

Exercise: shifting patterns

Sit comfortably in a chair and cross your arms in front of your chest. Now without looking down, uncross and cross your arms once again, with the opposite arm crossing on top this time. Notice your ability to do this and also register how comfortable or uncomfortable it is. If you repeat this several times, does it become easier? Now clasp your hands together and notice which thumb is on top. Reverse the entire thing, shifting not only to the other thumb being on top but all of your fingers repositioning. Again, notice your level of ability to do the task and your level of comfort. How many repetitions does it take to have it become familiar? Some research suggests that it take twenty-one repetitions to learn a new skill or break an old habit. What is your experience? In order to change anything, we must be willing to move through the stage of discomfort. Take time to examine your habits. How many of your thoughts have become habitual? Do you always drive to work taking the same route? Which foot do you put into your pants as you dress? Vary it and see what happens. Sit on the other side of the table. Sleep sideways or upside down. Have fun making up your own exercises for challenging and deposing entrenched habits.

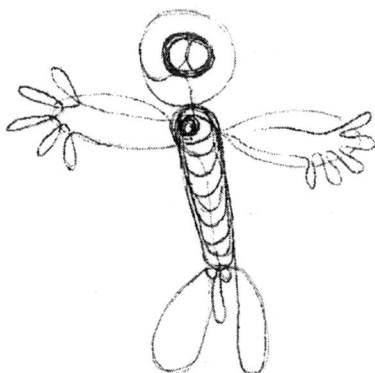

Whatever choice level – yin and yang, wrong lifetime incident, or sex mix-up – is not the issue. The acceptance of sexuality is positive if accepted; if unaccepted, it is experienced as painful and negative.

When the heart is in the wrong place, sex is overemphasized. Because of overemphasis of the two, physical discomfort causes ripple effects through the bodily functions. Removal from present influences, goals, and set-up is advised. Take a positive approach. The entity has to be able to feel good about itself before any change can occur. It takes a very evolved soul to make a positive out of the negative without incurring harm in the process and, through that process, 'stack up' karma.

These two writings once again remind us of the power of positivity and acceptance. They show that how we accept ourselves within our particular societal situations is of paramount importance. Today people are grappling with IQ versus EQ, our intelligence quotient versus our emotional quotient, and in many cases high EQ – a person with an outward expression of self-confidence and social know-how – will likely be more successful in life. Our self-assuredness and acceptance has direct bearing on whether we will create and function within a climate of comfort or disruption. The team reminds us that we are merely an expression of ourselves and of our perceptions.

Until I perceive, I cannot see;
Until I see, I cannot love as I would.

Predestination and personal will

We deliberated over whether or not this material should be in the chapter on reincarnation, but we felt (and the team confirmed) that though reincarnation is an important part of this material, it is clear that what we are now being shown is the role it plays in our growth and learning.

Often in this book, we have spoken of being placed in situations of discomfort, and perhaps this has been our required learning. Being led into the next edgy area is no exception to the trend. As we began to question the difference between learning and predestination, we realized that some of our best writings on the subject had emerged when we accessed our team for personal consultations on the topic of suicide or somebody's future. What follows are the team's answers to our questions given within the personal consultation, as well as the team's answer to the predominant question within the writing, 'What lies within my future?'

In regard to predestination and personal will, we discussed this when the issue arose about suicide. We might as well put a face on the whole soul aspect.

A person is going to be confronted with issues on the choice level as they are presented. Although a lifetime has been chosen on a karmic level to learn its lessons needed, this has always been done within the learning framework.

Predestination as a 'cast in stone' issue would automatically eliminate the learning and growth as part of the soul experience. Decision-making processes are based on personal growth, circumstances, and insight. Tears are shed and dried, and the hurt that caused them is given the memory we allow it. Learning, insofar as it has been caused by events, is the greatest gift to ourselves.

Within each person's lifetime, this is what directs us – with or without the karma or reincarnation belief system. Belief in reincarnation allows for gracious acceptance of our life cycle.

Decision-making?

A personal writing

When confronted with a question in regard to the future, the answer was quite simple: the entity has not made up its mind yet. The implication of this statement has a major impact upon the thought of predestination as previously perceived.

The unit of our individual soul has the overall effect of a totality; it has the ability to make decisions and changes, thus taking on a viability of its own.

The decision-making process of an entity takes in the complete realm of emotional culture and philosophy. The will both to live and to survive are the initial tools of functioning in this thought process. The entity takes it upon itself to undergo a new situation. Through the evaluation of the continuing process, it is in complete control of the route it decides to take. Although we can imagine the force of projection of the entity – or in other words, the effect upon its environment of the decisions it has made – we also have to consider the impact of the surroundings in which it has placed itself.

We can use the image of a ball bouncing off a wall, or the stones in a bag that will polish each other when jostled. Adhering to this thought for humankind, it stresses the knowledge that we must extend ourselves to our fellow beings. The responsibility of each person is that choices have to be made carefully.

Our life has not been cast, but it does have a choice of change.

Suicide

Acceptance of reincarnation opens us to the realization that suicide is merely a postponement of challenges to be conquered. While there is no hurry – we have eternity to work within – there are some issues to be considered.

In the first place, a desire to die can mean many things other than the physical death of the body. It can refer to the desire for the death as a way of being, or it can refer to a death of ego. It can also be an escape when the entity has overchallenged itself or underplanned for a particular karmic experience.

Whatever the underlying motive, a completed suicide will mean that the entity will return to similar karmic conditions in another lifetime.

The beauty of this writing on suicide is that it in no way lays any judgement or guilt upon the entity. Rather, it points once again to the role of personal choice. It does, however, clearly tell us that the unfinished business of a lifetime is inescapable and will have to be dealt with in subsequent existences. To those intrigued by goal setting, it could be noted that effective goal setting pays off in the in-between as well as the here and now. For further ruminations, please refer to the writing 'And life goes on' in chapter six.

Self-search, innate in every human,
tallies high in growth on the spiritual level.

Learning is ...

When this writing alludes to a 'happening of found trust', it could be speaking of the unexpected relaxed state the body experiences when a rightful decision is made. It alludes to a stream moving to unknown destinies, and of having the love and the trust to move along to a space that should be better. Sometimes such a move can be challenging and brings with it a level of discomfort because it leads us into unknown areas. This requires us to have a level of trust to allow for changes to occur. The importance of quiet is imperative. This writing gives us a thought worth pondering: 'The quality of the answers to our whys is determined by the depth of thought and clarity of the questions asked'.

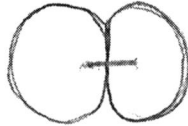

Learning is the thinking in the quiet and the coming to a decision – moving to poles till a balance exists, mirroring the image in a form which can be accepted. It is like the flow of a stream, which soothes the thought, the happening of found trust through a decision well made.

The mirror of the self is reflected by the background events of a part which did not work; the show of a stream which moves to unknown destinies; the love and trust to move along to a space which should be better.

Learning is done on the abstract level, which moves in quiet and needs to find the answer to questions yet unknown. Learning is in the answer to the why; the level is determined by the depth of the thought, clarity of the question, and reason beyond meaning.

Silence

In the quiet I hear more:
The sound of the waves,
The song of a rock.
In the quiet I hear more:

The secret of the pines,
The swish of butterfly wings in flight,
The hush of a feather falling.
In the quiet I hear more.

Chapter 10
Application, application, application

Practice makes perfect

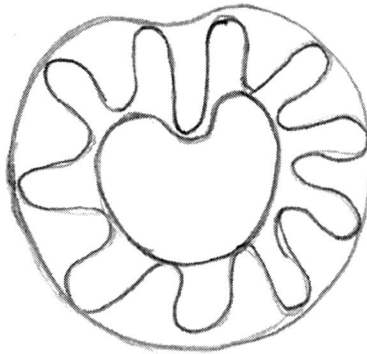

We are now moving into quintessential application, though it could be argued that reading this book is application in and of itself. In this respect, we speak of the writings and accompanying drawings which, when studied, have the ability to transport the reader into another dimension: a meditative state. Now, as we begin to put it all together, we make use of this foundational material and apply it to help unlock our uncharted corners of consciousness.

In subtitling this effort as a guidebook for personal and spiritual growth, we promised a how-to book, and this portion of the book can be seen as the dénouement, a tying together of the concepts that have been given, a toolkit for applying the ideas we have introduced.

Throughout this book, you have reflected on a series of recurrent themes and clues on how to unlock your own uncharted corners of consciousness. These include a willingness to both seek and develop a curiosity into what makes you function, a magnetic pull to connect with something larger than and outside of your personal self, and an acceptance that you are an active part of the process. Add to this some knowledge on clearing and quieting the mind and on attending to the needs of the body, and you are well on your path.

We were surprised that the team repeated the word 'application' three times. They had also repeated the word 'learning' three times in the previous chapter – was once not enough to show how important it is to apply what we have learned and to live to the utmost of our abilities? What we found was that repetition would be used as a powerful teaching tool. Our gearing in routine each time we sat down to work with the team proved to be very effective in focusing us and preparing us for our work. First we dealt with our day-to-day situations and, once discussed, put them to rest. We then made our cup of coffee, sat down, greeted and thanked the team, and began writing. Even the subject matter of the writings often repeated itself and then took us deeper. This repetition gave weight to what we have said throughout the exercises already given. The more you do them, the easier and more effective they will become. Without putting all of the information given into use, it would simply become theoretical naval gazing. Repeating 'application' three times was like the ringing of a school bell. Welcome to spiritual boot camp!

Many ideas will also be repeated throughout these application chapters, because the approaches and the conditions necessary for advancing into the realm of the spirit are themselves basic: slowing down, turning inward, focusing intention, and nurturing a positive attitude. You will be prodded to commit to the discipline of consistent repetition.

We accept that we are more than our physical presentation; *'we can so easily fall for the concept that we are merely our visible parts'*, and though these writings point to its importance, they caution us not to get bogged down in our everyday events. Rather, we should acknowledge our uniqueness and beauty, acknowledge that we are multifaceted like diamonds or crystal. We should clearly affirm that support, understanding, positive acceptance, and unconditional love are guidelines which will facilitate each person's ability to reach and draw from his or her own deeper and larger understanding. Much that is worth examining exists within a large grey area.

We will give you the tools to embark on an exploration of this grey area so that like archaeologists, you can sift through your personal layers and artefacts to gain access to the wealth contained within the storehouses of your uncharted corners – those corners unswept and unexplored.

The Same Old Story

The same story all over again.
Eve gave Adam the apple,
    the fruit of knowledge:
A metaphor which finds a parallel in these writings.
The body is the apple
    and the way it represents itself to us –
    the colour, size, and shape.
Superficially, it is how we represent ourselves.
On the outside, it shows the blemishes,
    and it perfectly depicts the impact
    the outside world has upon it.
Season and sun, water and food –
    a symbol that all has gone well or not.
That is the outside.

Then comes the flesh, the meat,
    the essence.
That is the nurturing part:
The part in each of us and the apple,
    which determines if we are palatable or productive,
    poisonous or destructive. In the body-soul-mind concept,
    we equate this with the mind part.

Mind is invisible;
    it is not a vehicle.
    Rather, it is a critical self-governing
    focus of the self.
Mind is an idea, a tool, a modus operandi.
Without the mind, without the flesh,
    without the meat, what are we?

A surface without a depth,
a window with nothing to look at,
a trip without a purpose.
The mind, as a tool, facilitates
the interaction of the soul with the surface.
It makes the surface, the appearance, have a reason
for being, a purpose for functioning,
a foundation for the effort
which goes beyond self-purpose and self-realization,
transmitting its DNA to a function
which is worth the effort.
The soul is our core;
it determines our range of capabilities
set according to a fixed rule,
which found its backing long ago.
While having a destiny of it own,
it is the connecting part
with all from which it came;
following a rule which was set in the past,
it can still grow to a uniqueness of its own.
Having the proper support and advantages,
it grows and blooms.
Having too many limitations, it will never have a chance.

Ponder on the lowness of the apple.
Ponder on the chain it signifies.
Rules of nature find many similarities among themselves,
and the axiom of being alive follows the same sequence.
A crystal is a form which nature has allowed.
Our body is a form which nurture has allowed,
with a range of its capacity
developed according to the laws of eternity:
The outside, the surface, is the shape we come in;
the exterior takes the impact of our surroundings.
This is the physical record of our travel.
The surface could be a reflection of surroundings
and the impact they had.

It is the mirror of what happened out there
      to what comes from in here.
Revealing and deceiving,
      it gives a picture with a warped scope.

The voice is one of the expressions of the inside.
Listen to the sound of what comes out.
Listen to the content.
Listen to the meaning.
Listen to the mind,
      which has a song of its own.
Listen to the sound of our inner voice;
      hear the song of the mind, knowing that:
                  The body is the what,
                  The mind the how,
                  And soul the why.

This writing uses poetic form and Adam and Eve's apple as a central metaphor for the whole entity. The body, that which reveals itself outwardly, is how the entity represents itself – is it perfect or blemished, productive or not? Along comes the *mind* to facilitate the connection between the body and its infuser. Mind facilitates *'the interaction of the soul with the surface'*. The mind is the tool determining how we function. Will we be palatable or productive, poisonous or destructive? With the presence of soul, we progress from skin deep to core. In the drawing, soul, our core, is represented by a heart. We are told it has a destiny of its own, set long ago in the in-between, an allusion to reincarnation. The metaphor continues: as with the wind and sun in nature, if conditions are right, the fruit will blossom and grow; if harsh, it will wither.

To unlock the whole picture, to see the whole person, to taste the true essence, as when we bite into an apple, we must take time to delve inward. Taking such time is the continuous thread, woven throughout the entire fabric of these application chapters. Taking time to stop our everyday activities; finding a place of comfort; slowing down; and quieting the body, the mind, and the emotions is essential. Only then can the probing begin.

We look at our surface, the physical, knowing it can reveal and deceive. Alternatively, we watch what happens when mind intervenes.

Mind promotes the interaction with that physical surface, giving it a purpose for functioning by accessing soul, while spirit continues to be the energizer. We can utilize clues offered by voice to view this interaction because voice is the outward expression of the inward.

Yes, it still is the same old story!
The body is the what, the mind the how, and the soul the why.
However, we are also a seed in the wind ...
and thank you
for not forgetting that you are also the kernel of a fruit.

Like all the writings, "The Same Old Story" can be used as a contemplative exercise to glimpse into the complexity of who we are. We offer two quite different exercises with which to work; see which one best suits your style and use one or both of them as you ponder on your essential Self.

Exercise: exploring the wonder of ourselves

Allow yourself to utilize the writing itself as your meditative exercise. Follow its directive and stop your everyday activities; find a place of comfort; slow down; quiet the body, mind, and emotions; and begin to ponder the wonder of who you are. We remind you that the 'progressive relaxation' and 'relaxing up' exercises are good ones to use for achieving quietness.

Who are you in all of your wonder and complexity? Where is your kernel? How do you link to the whole of creation? One of the ways these things became apparent to us and allowed us to find answers to these questions was by reviewing our own lives and noticing the paths we had chosen, the activities to which we were drawn, and the people to whom we gravitated. From this inventory of our outward, we began to notice our craving for things of the soul. Moving more inward, we sought more quiet time; Gerbrig went off on her boat for longer periods of time, and Shelly built a retreat place, her sacred space at the back of the garden. More and more, life itself became our meditation. Questions of a contemplative nature would arise from our solitary time and the time we spent together in study. We began to see ourselves as a part of our surroundings and appreciated the wonder of seeing all that we had been wishing for come into being. We experienced ourselves as a part of creation in all its forms through the creativity that came pulsing through us. We both began writing poetry, a smattering of which is in the book. Shelly completed an entire collection of children's poems and books, which have been submitted for publication. Gerbrig is completing her collection of poems. Our line of questioning shifted. 'What', we asked, 'of the magic of my thinking, my ability to solve issues as they arise? What is the sound of my heart beating?'

Allow all of your layers to reveal themselves in their miraculous beauty, and when you connect with this essential dimension, give thanks.

Exercise: merging your internal and external

Seat yourself comfortably in a chair with your spine straight; feel the support of the chair on which you sit. Use your breath to relax the body and allow your mind to release any distracting thoughts as though they were clouds floating away. From this place of relaxed alertness, allow a picture to form of yourself as you move around in the outside world. Be specific and let your picture be bright. Once you have the image and perhaps the feelings that accompany the image, see yourself placing all of the pictures and feelings into a large, clear cylinder and set the cylinder aside. Now allow a picture to form of your interior life and note the images and feelings associated with this place. When you are ready, again see yourself placing these images and feelings into a second large, clear cylinder and set that aside. Now take the two cylinders and imagine yourself pouring the contents of them into a third cylinder. Armed with this mixture, allow an image to emerge of your self moving through your day infused with the mix of interior and exterior life. How has your movement changed? What new qualities have you embraced? When you have this information, slowly and quietly open your eyes and begin to walk imbued with this new energy.

Taking a bite

These initial writings equate the entity with an apple's different layers and functions. They encourage us to look at different avenues for approaching this complexity – in chapter eleven we are encouraged to pay attention to bodily requirements: rest, the value of activity and exercise, and bodywork such as massage and energy work.

Energy work refers to therapies that address the energy field or unseen systems of the body, including the electromagnetic field surrounding our body (often called the auric field or aura). Some disciplines focus on the energetic meridians on the inside of the body. Therapeutic touch and polarity are the former – not touching the skin, but staying three to five inches above its surface. Hands-on work does make contact with the skin, though the focus of the treatments can be on the energy field inside, such as with shiatsu (which gets to the deeper Self through meditative exercises), tai chi, regression, and dream work.

Another approach is working through our senses, our windows into the world:

- sound: music uses the cadence of the music to synchronize body rhythms
- sight: mandalas use pictures to quiet our busy thoughts
- touch: hands-on bodywork strengthens our physical body
- taste: cleansing diets, herbal teas, and fasting removes impurities from the body
- smell: aromatherapy plays a role in bringing a feeling of well-being

Specific exercises for all of the above are provided in the exercises for chapters fourteen and fifteen.

Chakra work, which reaches within our energy centres and our astral and etheric beings, is closely related to or interrelated with many meditative approaches.

Given the diversity of instrumentation in the human condition, we realize a variety of approaches are necessary to honour the wide range of individual personality profiles. Therefore we encourage you to seek out and utilize that which makes your heart sing. This is indeed the ultimate exploration of your Self, which leads us to another essential thread in knowing you are on your way to self-discovery. If it feels good in the body, mind, and emotions, then it usually is. The opposite is equally true.

As entities, good nurturing supports us in expressing our full range of capabilities. Our outside, the shape we come in, takes the impact of our surroundings. It in turn reveals only what is happening outside, giving an incomplete or warped picture.

Shakespeare Revisited

Couplets captivate the mind,
Distracting true intent of line.
Softening many a heavy thought,
False levity thus is brought.
Cocktail party poetry
Masks our inner reality.

Chapter 11
Body the vehicle

A springboard to spirit

Body *is the vehicle,*
Mind *the driver,*
Soul *the infuser.*

In today's society, given the obsession with our bodies and how they look and function, it is almost an insult to say it is essential that our bodies be well maintained. But look at some of the ways we are flocking to maintain ourselves: applying veneers on our teeth, carrying borderline anorexic weights, injecting Botox into every apparent wrinkle, and indulging in cosmetic surgeries that stretch and tuck and slurp our unwanted fat to enhance our appearances. Can we really say we are

119

caring for our bodies? Certainly we are not always caring for ourselves as a totality. However the focus of this book is the freeing of consciousness and accessing the deeper dimensions, and within this context, body is important as our physical anchor. It gives us the capacity to maintain our footing in the physical world. Our focal point is to see body as the platform from which we can reach out and capture spirit, enabling it to permeate our daily lives. This vantage point has always been the impetus behind Shelly's work, both in her stress management business and Trager bodywork practice. We were delighted to see the issue of maintenance of body, and the good health bestowed upon it was dealt with in such depth in the following writings.

The body and well-being

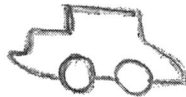

The body has been subscribed as being a vehicle moving, manipulating, and enabling; it is a mobile entity that allows us to function to the fullest. Many times we suggested the word 'vehicle' as a way of describing mobility in an understandable and workable form. Mobility is the locomotion of something, but using locomotion as a descriptor of one of the body's options doesn't adequately cover the degree of refunctioning or regeneration which is possible within our bodies. A vehicle of locomotion is a dead-end, functionality without regeneration. Our vehicular body is a mobile one, with the option for total function and regeneration.

We prefer the words regenerable or reparable because replenished cells do have the ability to renew themselves. While eventually doomed to self-destruct, we have the option to recharge and retool our physical instrument. We are the generators within our own creation.

Within the retooling, re-dyeing is the element of growth and learning. Does one want it, does one need it? It could behove both healer and healee to ask these questions. This leaves retool and re-die open to options. No work is undone by either the healer or healee.

We would like to take a moment to share once again with you the different ways we received our messages from the team. Sometimes we heard then speaking to us, the term for which is clair audial. Other times we saw the messages as we wrote them down or received the drawings, the term for which is clair visual. The third way of receiving our transmissions was just feeling them, a kind of kinaesthetic knowing which is said to be clair sensual.

After all the serious writings where body the physical is mentioned, we received this one that playfully discusses the body as a car. The metaphor extends itself into the realm of the technical with terms such as retooling, generator, repairable, and re-dyeing. Perhaps the team was alerting us to taking care of our body as we would a well-oiled machine.

We began to have fun. We realized there were two possible spellings for die – or was it dye? Because the word had come to us clair audially, it could be either.

We were stymied. Was the team talking about dye as it refers to a colour, or dye as in changing a particular colour or hue, which refers to our external persona? Or had they made reference to die as in 'the toss of the dice'? Perhaps it was the tool used for forming materials into shapes, as in 'the die is cast', to which they referred? Or were they alluding to our finite life when we take leave of the earthly plane, as in 'dead and gone'? As all of these options forced us to pay attention to the mechanics of our own body, we were reminded of its fragile and temporary nature.

We now turn the questioning back to you: What does your body represent to you? Why would 'subscribe' be used, when 'describe' would have been adequate? Is it because one term brings a subjective view, and the other an objective one? To use the term 'subscribe' can mean we accept an outward definition or interpretation of our bodies – for instance the fashion trends which tell us how we should look. Our way of working was to search for answers to all of the questions the team asked, carefully seeking a lesser-known interpretation. If the dictionary presented four definitions for the same word, and the first was the one we knew best, invariably the team would be talking about definition three or four. For this reason we have chosen to throw self-inquiry back at you, the reader, so that you can experience the delight of having your interpretations stretched. As we grappled with whether die or dye was the intended spelling, we concluded that die was correct because it had the element of change and choice, whereas dye was static and irrevocable.

At the end, the writing turned a different corner. It did not leave us in the parking lot to ponder, but rather it shifted gears. It finished with looking at the body as a machine. This way of looking at things opened up greater possibilities and responsibilities. Our body has autonomous locomotion, and unlike a car, we have some regenerative capabilities – a vehicle cannot regrow a bumper.

As we have said before, we are the generators within our own creation. These sayings clearly throw the responsibility of maintaining our vehicle back to us. We must take ownership of its well-being. There is a choice! We do have an opportunity to make our bodies places of comfort and protection.

Finally, the writing adds another car to our lot: the health care professional. It begins with a cautionary note: does the client want or need regeneration? A familiar warning followed by a familiar reassurance, 'No work is undone by either the healer or healee'. On the soul level, there is no right or wrong approach; all experiences are a part of growth. Some experiences are more comfortable than others, but is that necessarily good?

Having reassured us of the regenerative powers of the body-mind, we are reminded that there is purposefulness in working out the kinks, for they are a part of our earthly existence. In the words of the team,

If everything around you was working smoothly and without challenges, you would not be here; neither would we. There would be no bumps in the road for the vehicle to need watching. 'Re-dyeing is the element of growth and learning'.

This seemingly playful writing has a profound underpinning. It gave us a great deal of food for thought and occupied a considerable number of our study hours. It also reminded us that the seemingly simple mantra

Body *is the vehicle,*
Mind *the driver,*
Soul *the infuser.*

really is the central teaching and guiding principle of this book.

The body: active interventions

Growing into wholesomeness

There are many forms of active interventions aligning the body: enjoying a hobby, playing sports, visiting with friends, and starting an exercise program. All require a certain degree of discipline and demand the person to exert a certain amount of proactive control over his or her life.

The benefits of applying these active interventions are many. Besides altering established routines, one can fuel the body, work off excess energy, invigorate, build self-esteem, and afford sociability. Such pursuits are effective stress relievers. A case in point was Gerbrig's decision to live on a sailboat for twelve years. Because of a serious illness, she was forced to leave her job. After five years of regaining her health, and with life on the sea her husband's long held dream, they used this opportunity to trade in the security of life as landlubbers. He sold his business, they took off on their thirty-eight-foot sailboat, and they left friends and family behind. With only the two of them as crew, they established a new network of friends, saw sights unavailable to most conventional travellers, and accumulated enough adventures to take centre stage at any dinner party or exotic travel event. In Gerbrig's words, 'We didn't travel; the boat was our home, and the world traveled around us'. Sometimes their hitchhikers were butterflies, and other times they were birds. This time together certainly stretched them, allowing them to see and live in a variety of cultures on their terms. Remembering that this chapter is devoted to body, it is relevant to note that the ultimate bonus of Gerbrig's time spent on the boat was that she was able to regain her health and keep her autoimmune deficiency in remission. The experience permanently enriched their lives.

Similarly, Shelly attributes her ability to stay healthy to her Trager practice, which was and continues to be an antidote to her very active and committed day-to-day life.

Movement and posture are the physical expressions of a person. Years of habit-forming misalignment of self, outside influences, or simple misunderstanding of the place of the self in a larger dimension have not always allowed the person to express himself or herself in an unencumbered way. Exercise, movement, dancing, and physical participation with music have ways of aligning the unexpressed self with the wholesome function of Self.

A measure is to be made, a gradation given for the body, which is in essence on the front line of life. Not only does it do the dances, it also bows in supplication. It kneels in prayer and submits itself into devotions. It shows when it hungers in hard times or blossoms when cared for in good times.

When crouching in fear, with shyness in body lingo you should counteract it by rocking as if holding a child or like the dancing of the druids. This asks for confidence of the body, a willingness to participate with what happens around you, but it also allows joining in an energy form, which will enrich your confidence.

Bring the laughter back; give energy a boost and uplift confidence.

The previous writing uses the dance of the druids as a metaphor for disciplines and ritualized exercises (such as yoga, tai chi, Sufi dancing, Feldenkrais, walking the lines of a labyrinth or mandala, and the formalized cultural dances practiced by many peoples in ceremony and ritualized celebration). Through specified and repetitive movements, they facilitate a different, more meditative state of mind, which enhances a person's feeling of belonging to and connecting with a different dimension of themselves.

Through obliteration of the physical, they actively access those less-charted corners of our consciousness. All of these beg active participation on the part of the person.

Devotional practices of supplication and bowing can also be pathways to realignment.

In fact, for many ritualized dances, such as those of the First Nations People, preparation in the form of prayers and fasting precedes the actual dance. Walking down the aisle in a marriage ceremony carries the same impact – what seems common to all is the deliberateness of intention all require.

Body-passive interventions

Passive interventions include sleep, television, soaking in a bath, progressive relaxation, meditation, visualization, and bodywork. Bodywork works well for Shelly, as does visualization and being outside. Though television is not a preferred thing for her, movies are. Gerbrig loves being in nature and listening to and playing music. Sleep has been a powerful healer for both of us. Note that television and meditation are two distinct rungs on the ladder of relaxation. With meditation, the mind empties and the brain can be at rest. With television, we are not so empty; we use it to escape from a focused mind, but we recognize that we are still being bombarded by stimuli, white noise, or light. In fact, Marshall McLuhan's concept of the global village, in *The Medium Is the Message,* shows how television can take us out into the far reaches of the world. Perhaps it should be used as a motivator for social action. We do not, for instance, recommend watching the world news before bed, as it does little to enhance pleasant thoughts and dreams. We encourage you to pay attention to what works: action and stimuli to escape the day's realities as a way to relax, or soothing content to set a relaxed tone.

Reminder

Sometimes when I think I've forgotten,
My body remembers;
A smell, a touch, a hint of colour,
Waves of recollection –
Mine alone to understand.

The actual tissues of the body are a remarkable receptacle for both good and bad information. The invitation to understand this information can prove critical to our personal balance and well-being. Though the remembrance of a soft, supportive event can be soothing and even healthy, recollection of past horrors can hold us captive and render us immobile, unable to move forward in any positive way.

The unconscious mind often stores data and releases the conscious mind from the possibility of trauma triggered by replaying events such as rape, abuse, incest, and other violent acts. Recall and regressions often occur when the person has engaged in some form of unlocking, such as bodywork – a useful process, because the events can be reviewed with a trained person whose focus is on healing. See Chapter 4 The Whole in One Page 34, for a more detailed description of Bodywork

Turmoil caused by previous painful experiences often comes about when we listen to music of a sentimental nature, as portrayed in the poetry above. Nevertheless, our memory buttons can be triggered by any sensory experience. Stay closely tuned to the information received through the body and emotional responses – the feedback loop, rich in information on the self.

No-nonsense writing: R & R

We call this our no-nonsense writing. The abrupt tone still surprised us. Many words and phrases were strong: 'malice', 'hideous', and 'overt demands on our time'. It seems that we needed to be jarred. We were becoming complacent towards the interlopers and detractors in our environment, which have slowly and insidiously changed us: the faster pace of life, the increased stimuli. The writing pinpoints situations that have become so much a part of modern life, we miss that they are potentially harmful.

'Relax' is turning back into a lax or soft state.

'Unwind' is returning from a wound-up place.

Relax and unwind is so often heard of nowadays. Natural as it seems, it does not find a place within a normal functioning. Conditioned by a society which seems to accept a high stress level as normal, in order to willingly eliminate this stress we will have to notice and identify its origin.

Notice the malice in our everyday living: regimentation and overburdening of tasks and obligation. As never before we seem to be in a treadmill of functions and repercussions – examine them and kiss them good-bye.

Identify the many small, hideous, and overt demands on our time. Realize the pacing of body rhythms to speeds unknown before. Time and space are regimented to a pace which disrupts the more normal functions.

Presenting this in table form adheres to how the team first presented us with this material. Perhaps it was their way of highlighting.

Pace:	*TV viewed in space and time limits – the fifteen-second commercials*
	Horse buggies … time stood still
	Old movie … too long winded
	Narrative telling … get to the point
Tremor:	*Music … beat loud and overpowering*
	Cities … drone of sound day and night

Life is loud, time is money, and we are in it, a part of it all. Notice and identify, and know you are part of it. Now deal with it. It also hands this generation a vibration so unique as not to let this opportunity go to waste. It will teach us how to plan, make decisions, and go about it – and faster than before. A dynamic attitude with great energy has made us able to achieve states previously unheralded. To be aware of the potential of achievement depends on our ability to overcome the obvious drawbacks. In addition, here knowledge is wisdom.

Recognition of the potential within is part of the fine-tuning of the instrument (body). The more finely tuned and calibrated the instrument, the more effective it is. Notice and identify your stress and pressures, the ones around you and the ones particularly yours. Find ways to eliminate them regularly, when needed. The more one is adept in doing this at will, the more one's elasticity is increased.

Retreat from your environment – for shorter and longer periods – to facilitate a shift in yourself. This can be accomplished through walks, holidays, and a variety of activities which you the individual find pleasurable. Retreat from yourself – disengage body from the mind.

Facilitate the soul level to function without the burden of the heavy vibration of the body. This can be accomplished through sleep versus meditation. Rise above the din of living without being afraid to be part of it.

Dulled

Subway faces
Buried in books
Reflect the humdrum of the city

Exercise: a safe place

Sit comfortably in a chair with spine straight and feet touching the ground. Feel yourself supported by the chair. Close your eyes and allow yourself to go to a place (real or imagined) where you feel comfortable, safe, and supported: a beach, a mountaintop, a meadow, or a house you knew from childhood.

If you see a picture, make that picture bright; if you hear sounds or notice smells, take them in; if you feel something, let that feeling permeate your whole being. Take time to experience this special place, one to which you can return whenever you need it. You might like to gently press the side of your knee, the spot between your thumb and second finger, or tug gently on your ear lobe, to give yourself a physical anchor that will allow you to recreate this experience.

Look around: Is there is an object or a quality that attracts your attention? It could be a beautiful stone or crystal or flower, or it may simply be a quality like peace or love. If you have an object, see yourself picking it up and absorbing its strength and beauty. If it is a quality, let it flood your body.

Now it is time to leave your special place. Take the quality or object with you, knowing that they will help you to return here when you need solace. Slowly open your eyes, bringing the feeling you have experienced with you into the room.

This exercise is useful in creating a place of retreat that replenishes and refreshes you. If you repeat this exercise many times, you will eventually be able to retrieve your special place by simply taking a deep breath and thinking about it or by pressing on your physical anchor. It works well to begin with the progressive relaxation and then to proceed into this exercise.

Exercise: sequence in slow motion

Imagine there is a teacup on a tray, resting on the ground in front of your feet. You are going to bend down to pick it up, set it on your lap, take a drink, and then set it back down on the floor – all in slow motion. Take as long as you are able, and if possible, time yourself as you do the exercise. At the end of the exercise, notice your responses. Was it frustrating? Did the time seem longer than it actually was? Was it a refreshing change?

This exercise counteracts life's fast pace by slowing yourself down. You can apply this slow movement to many of your everyday activities, such as getting ready for bed. Be fully aware of every move you make and do each one with deliberation. Who knows? Maybe this pace could become addictive.

The body and its signals

Balm

Life's mysteries unfold through our pain.
Pleasure keeps our secrets neatly wrapped.

As the poetic fragment above suggests, life's most painful moments can catapult us into periods of great learning. Once there, we are forced to call upon all our resources, often treading far into uncharted waters – a

129

powerful and challenging place to be. This oft-used trick of snagging our attention through discomfort is an effective way the body speaks to us. If we are willing to notice and work with these disruptions, we have the opportunity to change the physical conditions and eventually develop the ability to catch these subtle signs early. In doing this, we learn to listen to the body's signals and to follow its wise knowing. This is perhaps the most important anti-stress technique possible: preventative behaviours. Once noticed and altered, dis-eases need not balloon into major disease; it is far better to catch the repetitive flutters in our chest or the butterflies in our stomach, changing our eating patterns or introducing exercise and meditation into our life immediately, than to wait and be motivated to do so by a heart attack or an ulcer.

Sometimes we do listen to the body, despite the fact that the mind is trying to dissuade us.

Be Yourself?

An unexpected invitation,
A physical response;
My body says yes.
I must go.
My mind leaps in
A battle of self-doubt.
You mustn't, you couldn't, you shouldn't.
I did.

Chapter 12
Mind the driver

Friend or foe?

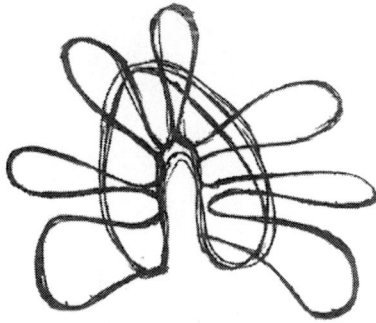

What began as almost a self-imposed obligation to work with this material became an extraordinary gift. It taught us to go one step farther than a course in psychology might. The teachings brought into our awareness the aspect of mind as driver, which spoke not of its motivational character enabling us to meet our life goals, but rather its role in bringing our transpersonal qualities forward, those qualities that are aligned with selfless service. The effect was profound. We began to look at ourselves and the people around us in a different, more peaceful, and less conflict-oriented manner. We also started to question our social obligations. Early on we became involved with meditation groups and started teaching it ourselves. When life presented some major curve balls – family illness, financial challenges, and more – we handled the situations from a broader, more spiritual perspective. An analogy could be that mind has the ability to send us to the library to take out a book, but mind also can go a step further and decide the nature of the book we choose. We were being urged to pick the ones about growing spiritually. Regardless of what turmoil or celebration was going on in our daily lives, our study time required us to detach from all of that, clear our minds, and enter into a contemplative space of receptivity and gratitude. Our lives were so enriched!

By now it is clear that mind propels our physical being; it is the driver and makes our physical life happen. While thinking can be seen as an internal process, we know that it also has bearing on even our outward postures. In this context, mind is also the interpreter – happy, sad, silly, mad, beautiful, ugly, fat, or thin. Our mind takes our daily interactions and puts them into a storyline. We then live our life driven by how we see ourselves. Self-knowledge becomes an important ally, a key component in determining whether mind becomes friend or foe. With self-knowledge at the wheel, we can career back into old patterns or veer away from outdated belief systems and steer towards new directions and behaviours. We are reminded of the team's beautiful teaching:

We live within and through our mindset, creating our own scenario. We are in essence our own masters.

Exercise: the close relationship of mind and body – a demonstration

This exercise can be done with eyes open or closed. Take a deep breath, clear your thoughts as best you can, think of your favourite food or meal, and imagine yourself eating it right now. If you are visual, picture it and let it be specific and bright. If you are more kinaesthetic, feel yourself eating that meal. Take a few moments to do this. Did you salivate when you imagined eating your favourite food? Could you actually taste or smell the food?

This exercise teaches us to be responsive rather than reactive. If we are conscious of our responses, we can use them to our advantage; if the responses are unconscious, they can use us without us being aware of them doing so. This is the mind-body in direct interaction. Just thinking brought forward a physical response.

In exploring this dimension of interconnectedness between body-mind, mind-body, body-emotion, and emotion-mind, we enter into the arena of self-health and self-care – a theme that will recur throughout this section.

The human body is actually a body and mind at the same time. You cannot separate the two, as these next exercises demonstrate.

Exercise: attitudes and physiology interacting

Stand up and hunch your shoulders forward. Cast your eyes down and notice how you feel. Is your breathing constricted? Does your chest feel caved in? Is this not the posture of a defeated or depressed attitude? From this position, it is impossible to feel positive.

Reverse that position. Thrust your shoulders back and lift your eyes upward – and suddenly everything shifts. The breathing is freer, and your perspective is outward looking. Your attitude is more positive. Do you feel you have more energy? Even if depressed, if you smile you will not be able to hold on to your low feelings.

A change in posture or facial expression can drastically affect your frame of mind, and how you are perceived by others is also affected. This in turn cycles back to you and affects your interactions with the world around you.

The deliberateness of mind

This writing refers to keeping the mind active and avoiding repetitive behaviours, treading the beaten path. So often we are trapped in our ideas and concepts, re playing old tapes which have little merit or relevance to our present circumstances. Yet to be snagged such thwarts our creativity and ability to be clear in our decision-making. Avoiding this trap requires attentiveness. The mind must be nurtured in order to develop and grow; otherwise it is merely an empty vessel, a receptacle with no agenda or attachment to outcomes.

As ever-changing people in a dynamic and evolving world, we must continually work to stay open, flexible, unencumbered, and free from routine behaviours and thinking. Situations that can most easily snag us are those which are closest to our heart, such as traumas or losses involving members of our immediate family, or unfortunate childhood experiences. Although this detachment is sometimes hard, it will still serve us better to strive for a clear mind. One of the ways of doing this is to approach life from a vantage point of not knowing – a place of emptiness and curiosity. This can be a difficult task in a busy world, which rewards us for continually knowing and doing more. Deliberateness is required to slow down and empty out. Often when we do this, we can be labelled boring. Yet this is the first step in achieving clarity and in accessing your deeper dimensions. Dare to be boring!

As we have previously mentioned, in the physical world curiosity, learning, and staying abreast of whatever is going on allows us to keep an active mind with a capacity to draw out of a big bag. On a spiritual level, it is quietness and being an empty vessel which allows the mind its freedom to roam in the realm of deeper thought. People are known to use just a small percentage of their mind potential, and creative thought is often drowned out through repetition on the beaten path.

Expanding your repertoire: challenging your repetitive behaviours

Determine how you most readily accumulate knowledge and commit to practicing the opposite. If you are comfortable poring over the works of eminent and erudite philosophers, set out for the great outdoors. For Shelly, reading the newspaper is a digression because it is not her preferred way of getting the news. Alternatively, Gerbrig is a voracious reader and is accustomed to checking books out of the library; she had to settle for any books that came her way during the twelve years she spent on the boat. Silence your mind, sharpen your senses, and prepare to see all you can. Learn by taking time to both hold and examine natural objects. Remember when you were a young child, when your most effective way to learn and to know was to pick an object up and often even to taste it. Become that infant again; though you likely do not need to taste sand, do allow yourself to explore texture and smell. See what you can discover.

On the other hand, if this modus operandi is old, challenge yourself to explore materials outside your usual purview. If the scientific has long been a fascination, begin to delve into the writings of teachers from the aboriginal disciplines: Native American, Hawaiian, Maori, or Ancient Egyptian. If these are well-known to you, look to bridging old and new. New hobbies and pursuits could emerge that you had never imagined doing. Challenge yourself in everyday occurrences: if you use your right hand to undertake simple tasks such as buttoning your shirt, try your left. If you're used to being the first one to offer an insight or opinion in conversation, instead become the listener.

Recent research has substantiated the importance of such practices. In doing old things in useful and new ways, we are forcing the brain to work with new patterns, which in turn stimulates the nerve endings to make new connections (increasing the synapses). You will expand the repertoire of your brain. The base of our physical existence is body and mind. Mental and physical viability are the keystones of our integral Self, and so without proper grounding of body and mind, our integral Self is highly disadvantaged. Alternatively, proper grounding moves us directly into the integration of body, mind, and soul; it is a gateway to the integral Self and spirit. In learning something anew, there is often a slight feeling of discomfort. Disturb the comfort and comfort the disturbed.

Selective memory

This writing reminds us of the need to be deliberate and conscious of what we record – another strong case for mindfulness, an essential step in accessing our soul dimension.

Selective memory is the part of our experience after it has filtered through the awareness of the individual. Every event enters our mind through the short-term memory, and if registered as being important enough, it is solidified in the long-term memory where it can be retrieved at will. Unless this information is recaptured, it will drift away into unconsciousness also to be forgotten. Our functioning and capacity to interact is always based on previously received and integrated information, but only our retrievable information is put into our conscious memory. One's inclination to decide what is important or not will determine how that individual will express himself or herself in the world at large.

Mind: a gateway to spirit

Attending to mind

This writing alludes to manifest, which is a lyric term given to any established thought to which we cling. Having cut into the sacred cow in our look at soul mates, in this section we put a further slice into the realm of yet another: the much venerated logical mind, sometimes called the right brain. The right brain is the home of linear thinking, our mental, social, and behavioural intelligence. Though we in no way negate its importance, as said in the last writing, the brain cannot be separated from the wholeness of our being. Nevertheless, we do allot it its place. For in the search into our uncharted corners of consciousness, this aspect should be left in the pen, so to speak, and the right brain should be released to roam free because it is the realm of intuitive sensing, feelings, and meditative thought that will shed light into those lesser-known corners, those spaces of expanded awareness.

Unfortunately, left brain does not answer to the laws of logic as we know them in the physical, though indeed it has logic of its own. It is a place where we meet ourselves on a completely different dimension. There are many doors of access to this place: meditation, hypnosis, dream work, and regression. It is sometimes unexpectedly forced open through trauma. However, the first step to opening the door is to slow down and clear the mind. This principle is true in all learning situations. The insights given in the writing are important for us to understand personally and for professionals in the therapeutic or supportive fields. Bringing our thoughts manifest into consciousness and examining them is truly our journey into our self-search, and it is the raison d'être of the book.

The mind draws from a wide range of capabilities which are either physically or spiritually based. This pool has been long established over countless lifetimes. Because it is intrinsically helpful to do so, in this lifetime the mind also goes through the various stages of conditioning, from learning and observation to social and cultural conditioning.

The mind may have been hampered through neglect and deprivation – the how and why is thus based on our cultural response to the thought manifest. Thought manifest is nothing more than giving a personal meaning and response to whatever is the original thought-form. Our social and cultural conditioning overlays the thought manifest so that it deepens and magnifies. It has thus assumed a form which takes on a personal aspect in each of us. By giving a purely physical interpretation to the events, it answers in clarity about the mainly physical aspect within the questioning individual; we find the same answers in giving it a spiritual response. Life, though, has and is being lived within our physical confines and based on higher motivation. Clear separation of these two should be acknowledged, even though there really is no separation. Daily interaction fluctuates constantly between the demands of either one plane or the other. Both need a certain flexibility to function within the other area.

Awareness, joy, confidence, and lack of fixation should enable us to be finely absorbed into interest in one specific arena, but with the conscious disallowance of the other. On the choice level, they both need understanding and sympathy. In body-mind-soul interaction, we function at our best with the full integration of these dimensions. When flexibility is diminished to a limited range, the entity is cut down to a dialogue with the self – a monologue on a different level. Movement out of this situation is done when decided by the entity. One needs protection and understanding to facilitate such a movement.

For fresh information to enter, space must be cleared in the mind. This point is illustrated by the story passed down from one generation to the next, a well-known teaching of the student who came to study with a Zen master. Eager to begin, the student sat impatiently waiting to be taught. 'First', says the master, 'we will have tea'. The master fills the cup to overflow and continues to pour as the tea brims over.

'Master!' cries the amazed student, 'why do you continue to pour when the cup is already full?'

'I would ask the same of you', replied the master. 'Why do you come to me for teaching when your mind is already full? First you must clear the mind; then we can begin'.

Adding the components of openness, quiet, and space allows new understandings to emerge that can also contribute to our mental, emotional, and physical well-being. We could ask, 'Are we *mind full* or *mindful?*'

Exercise: contracting for quiet –
a dialogue with your mind

Seat yourself in a quiet place. Ensure you are comfortable and close your eyes. Notice the state of your mind: is it brimming, full of thoughts and images? Make an agreement for quiet time with your active mind by imagining that you are placing all busy thoughts into a box and setting the box aside to be opened later. It is important to agree upon the time of opening; for example, 'I will get back to you in twenty minutes'. Without this contract, it may be hard for the mind to find comfort in quiet. This is particularly useful for those with an active mind that never stops; this simple exercise can be used to settle and rest it in order to set the proper tone for preparing for meditation.

Mind: friend or foe

The writing above deals with the fact that thought manifest can work to our advantage or disadvantage depending on how clear we are in our dealings with its parameters. The mind could be our foe because it can trap us in its clutches of wants and needs which may not serve our soul direction. On the other hand, it can also work to place us in alignment with our deeper purpose – if we are applying it with deliberateness.

Thought manifest revisited

In thought manifest the mind can be the fooler, trapped in its own lies. A very dicey remark because this so obviously ignores the possibility of its positive side. Thought manifest, in itself, describes an event that is unlikely to happen – wishful thinking at its best. It could be positive or negative, but in the above sentence (mind as the fooler), we like to think of it as a result of 'I want this', 'I like that', giving a false security of omnipotence, regardless of unforeseen circumstances – the castle in Spain, so to say. A positive manifest considers goal setting with a calculation of possible implications either for the person or others. Perhaps the work of this section is to clarify how not to be snared by the fooler.

Anecdotal writing: boxed in

The following was a personal consultation for a man who was caught in the trap of an overly focused mind.

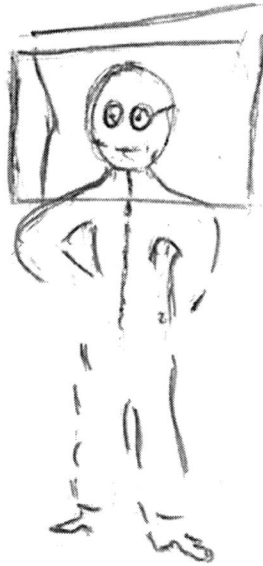

Emphasis is on life lived from the top down. Mental capacities and emotional functioning form the overtones towards the physical. Need of security and clothing, emphasized within the physical part of the self, are the protective feature of this essence. Recognition of these features could lead to acknowledgement of the role.

Overemphasis of cerebral function of this person shows strength within the physical functioning. Knowing the importance of where one's strength lies belies the draining into energies, which are supportive to the essence. Give understanding to the physical but allow the fullness to function.

Life in its essence has to be led as if fulfilling a determined task. Acknowledge the features through which we function, and a full benefit can be derived according to one's goal. Understanding and wisdom derived through the eons are features gained to be used. The acquiring of giving and sharing with mankind is acknowledging that essence is a gift to be shared.

The life one lives within the mode of maintenance is like working on the suit and not seeing the man.

The following are additional comments from our team, which we felt fit in well with the message of the previous writing.

The culmination of a lifetime is not judged by the achievements and experiences that were a part of it but, how all these have integrated into the self and the ability to enjoy and utilize them as a part of you. The ability to enjoy the fruits of one's labour, physically and emotionally, is the greatest deed of all.

This writing is a plea not to be stuck in the reverence of the body or mind, but rather to allow the wisdom of the soul to emerge. It is, in a sense, a warning not to stay in the outer layers – the suit, the realm of maintenance and security gathering. This is a plea to utilize the accumulated knowledge of the soul and its essence, and to cycle them.

Next is a commentary on how thought manifest is in essence the pets and peeves of our mind, those parts we have to overcome. We must, in the body, drop our conditioned movement patterns; in the mind, it is the beliefs we must question.

Belief systems – the foolers?

This writing could be seen either as an admonishment for worry and other projected fears or as an advertisement for living in the present. Deal with what is in front of you; to do otherwise accomplishes nothing. Like the proverbial rocking chair, you expend a lot of energy but do not go anywhere. Global disruption may or may not happen, but worrying about it will not help. What will help us is coping with the circumstances as they occur and by making changes accordingly, rather than missing the experiences of the moment.

As the connection to the spiritual aspect of our being develops and grows, beliefs impede the process, and they should be examined and dropped where necessary. Beliefs shape our perception of the world and others and are the basis of selective attention and self-fulfilling prophecies. If we believe the G-dhead is a powerful, punishing father figure, this is what we will experience. If we believe we are bad people, we will not notice or integrate positive feedback. Our ability to create our life space is astoundingly competent and accurately reflects the belief systems we hold. What you focus on is what you create.

An excellent example is foreboding. Foreboding is a personal concept regarding the future. The future takes care of itself. The foreboding concept is a translation through one's own mind. Dealing with the present, although hard, is reality. Foreboding is not real; it is just a thought.

For example, take global disruption. Global disruption does not extend past an individual's perception of his or her immediate surroundings. Global thought, a burden taken on, has to be seen as an extended thought pattern with emotional overtones beyond one's own feelings, an exaggeration of thought which is self-induced.

Carpe Diem

Expectations,
Anticipations
Rob us of our todays
By promises of tomorrow.

As we leave this chapter on mind, having scrutinized its potentials and drawbacks, we acknowledge once again that a well-functioning body and mind are the avenues necessary for the emergence of the expression of the soul.

Chapter 13
Soul the infuser

Are we more than our physical container?

Soul, the infuser, is an unconditional space within the Self that feels one with all, where blaming and resentment are unknown and material issues find no place: our place of deeper thought, of poetry and creativity, of unconditional acceptance of self and others.

This certainly struck us as a big assignment given the fact that gossip and self-comparison are such easy traps to fall in at any stage, but as mothers of teens, how tempting! 'My child was so amazing on the

basketball court today, and you should see my child's science project …'
In those times, carpooling was the central task of the day, and the time
to write poetry or design the latest pattern for a sweater took a back seat
to packing lunches and after-school snacks.

Accessing the unseen

*Discussions dealing with the uncharted corners of consciousness have led us
full circle. We discussed in general terms the higher Self, described planes or
astral levels, and subsequently delved into the body and its functioning on
a non-medical level. Presently we continue with ways to access the unseen
part of our self, our deeper function and soul level, and work with the notion
of how all those interact. Tools and means, support and personal struggle set
aside, we maintain the only option not expressed: the notion of choice.*

*The complex interaction of our different levels, stages, needs, and wants
is in constant eternal flux. Here is another way of describing soul growth in
everyday terms:*

Love Is Living

Life is learning;
Soul is projecting
A need in all.
Heart is giving;
Want is taking;
Greed is the fall.

Mood is changing,
Heart placating,
Living all the life.
Greed not wanting,
Taste to curbing;
What is all, our call.

Love is living
in the giving

> *of the full and want*
> *to the sharing*
> *of the caring*
> *in the great*
> *All.*

Stretching consciousness

Every time we worked with the team, we were stretching our consciousness. They forced us to leave the immediacy of the events of our lives and dedicate ourselves fully to our course of study. Our intensely busy lives – juggling work, carpools, and community commitments – did not always make this retreat into study easy. It was like doing mental yoga, and we didn't even have the comfort of saying, 'I've gone back to school to do a degree in education'.

Expanded awareness or altered state awareness is seen as an extension of normal awareness. Normal awareness is awareness as seen in situations that present themselves to the observer through those of our senses whose functions can be clinically observed.

The altered state of awareness mainly deals with senses and perceptions that are excluded from the nervous tactile function of the human state. The altered state of consciousness is the situation in which one finds oneself if and when normal, everyday perception is changed to exclude the direct observant consciousness.

An expanded awareness, however, refers to the extension of conscious awareness and utilizes in everyday functioning the perceptions of altered awareness as presented in a meditative state.

The functions of the brain are influenced by the state they are in. Alpha is a state of total 'here awareness', beta a twilight or half sleep state, and delta the deep sleep state. These physical and mental states are recognizable in the brainwave pattern because they can be observed through the electro-encephalogram. Total awareness can only be achieved within the alpha state.

Right brain deductive thinking, which functions through selective fact-finding procedures, is combined with the mental capacity, which is based on learned behaviour, mental deduction, or knowledge.

Information, which eventually coded itself as retrievable knowledge in the grey matter of the brain (reactivated through use and laid down in change of thought-to-be reused and superfluous information), is dropped.

Total awareness, therefore, involves allowing the insight gained in altered states to be recalled in normal awareness and to become available for use in everyday life. Practice of this process eventually allows fluid access to right brain meditative awareness while maintaining ordinary consciousness.

Airborne

To view the mountains from the air
gives rise to unlinked imagery
confounding the linear mind.
Open stretches, dusted white peaks,
taupe coloured origami,
potter's clay waiting to be fashioned.
Fields become mosaics-spirals, diamonds, squares,
patterns, and patchwork,
a collage.
What is big appears small;
what is small shrinks and disappears.
The plane, a small tin container, suspended.

Exercise: a different view

Like our view from the plane, we are often able to gain a different perspective. Something as simple as a change of position, distance, or direction is often the catalyst that enables us to see things differently. For the purpose of this exercise, be willing to explore and to change position. Possibly a new vantage point will emerge to allow yourself to let go and to be open to new experiences.

1. Help to bring the meditative state into your day-to-day reality by changing your habitual, everyday behaviours.
2. Experiment with your wardrobe and design a new you. If blue is your favourite colour, wear red.

3. Finger paint; explore shape, texture, and colour by making a collage; and then find aspects of yourself within that collage. The results are guaranteed to surprise and could make some permanent changes you like. The child in you could be freed.

Soul purpose: accepting responsibility

On the soul level man knows all; on the earth level the choice might be simplicity.

Finding our purpose

This writing is a calling to put what you know to use. Although it suggests that we have been encouraged to let go of established patterns, there is a further step we can take to affect change. We must step outside our established way of thinking in order to free ourselves from the clichés of our daily lives. Because times can be so difficult, in order to cope we will need to access the knowledge that is available only from the level of the divine. Though they say it may not be easy to deal with what accompanies our changes, the team urge us not to 'punch out'. And as always, though there is an acknowledgement that a tooling of the self is required for access, finally there is recognition that there is an element of deliberate choice on the soul level. This thought is housed in the statement 'it took courage to incarnate', and 'many of you souls came to help' certainly speaks of a reason for being here. And just in case we haven't been prodded enough to accept responsibility on the transpersonal plane, there is a 'PS' that says, 'Don't think soul age can be used as an excuse'. There is equal opportunity for all ages.

An increased quickening of the learning and changing vibration has made it necessary to access knowledge inspired on the divinity level. Tooling of the self will be necessary to breach both a gap and time, which will be increasingly tiresome. It is easy to give up, break down, or punch out altogether; we do not want that because it took courage to incarnate. Many of you souls came to help.

PS from the soul level: The concept of younger souls or older souls is nonsense. The soul is eternal; it will never be young or old. Only learning is graduated because it follows a path.

Responding to the deeper calling

In all veracity we can say we were never resistant to the deeper calling. Rather we were curious, and this curiosity kept us engaged. It felt like a coming home, like we were dialoguing with old friends. We were eager to find the time we needed to work and learn together. Though ours was an easy relationship, the writings often threw us for a loop; it was as though the team was making sport.

We place so many expectations on ourselves as to how things will unfold, and in so doing we miss the unfolding. Forget the dramas of day-to-day, for they are there merely to catch our attention, and they afford only a brief glance to glamour. How much richer to enter into the quiet and seek for that which is within – untouched by all that surrounds. The soul cares little for the outer wrappings; it cares only to carry out its service and will push hard to be heard. That the pushing can take the form of discomforts is reasonable, because otherwise we stay in the realm of what is known. Therefore, we find ourselves at moments of growth appearing to do otherwise: appearing at a standstill, appearing stuck, appearing non-productive ... simply appearing. But the real show – that which will appear – can come only from within. Is not the eye of the storm the centre? No fuss, no fume, no flash, just a deep pool of profundity. For indeed we are led further and further within, spiralling to our very core where creativity dwells. This is the great paradox so long taught:

> *We do without doing,*
> *Know without knowing,*
> *Find without seeking.*

In accessing our deeper dimensions we must first spiral into the depth of our personal being; our centre, a unifying metaphor, has been used throughout this chapter on soul: the spiral. Then when we reach our place of stillness, we spiral back up and out to link with the All. The writing makes a connection between creativity and our core. Finally, it is acknowledged that in this process of delving deeply, we can access our creative dimensions and open ourselves up to a way of being so different from how we were before.

Direct dialling:
connecting with your spiritual teaching team

Garbled? Unclear? Getting clearer? Clarifying? At first, these small writings were not easy to grasp. Gradually we realized the team used metaphors and analogies from the communication field. Often it felt like the information came in telegram style. We could say our team asked us to stay tuned while the static cleared. And we did just that. These initial training sessions with our spiritual teaching team required a stick-to-it attitude on our part and a belief that there was really something in all of this, that we weren't just crazy – but it wasn't always easy. We needed to trust that despite static on the lines, and even in times of complete disconnect, we could stay in touch with our higher dimensions. Out of sight was not necessarily out of reach.

We struggled in the beginning, because the teaching style of the team was often to throw us off-kilter, create an imbalance in order to bring us to a more balanced place – *'confounding the linear mind'*. When we sat down for our weekly sessions, we never knew what challenges were in store for us: the language used or the concepts presented (which were not a part of our everyday focus). Then came the messages on our potential and purpose. Write a book? We were busy homemakers, not authors. But we did stay tuned, and the static did clear as we continued to dial up and dig deeper. And here we are today, completing the final chapters of this book. As we explained in our introduction, in those initial sessions, we were carefully coached, and we in turn became fully committed to the process. It was evident we were not alone, yet it was also obvious was that we were fully engaged in a course of study. And so these writings, though initially intended for us alone, apply to all. As we said in the preface, we all have the ability to access our teams and to work with them to do the work our individual souls have chosen to do. And how can one come to know what that work is? The directives contained in the writing 'Direct dialling' a bit further on in this chapter, sheds some light on how our team understood these temptations and continued our spiritual training process in earnest but in a very down to earth, everyday manner. They used the metaphor of technology and told us how to tune in and turn on.

Like one's initial experience with e-mail, when we were first brought online with our spiritual teaching team, our efforts were crude and haphazard. However, as our lessons continued, they taught us to gain a greater ease of access, which the team called 'direct dialling' or 'hi-fi'. Once again, we were both applauded and admonished for our efforts, but in time we came to understand that hi-fi was really an attitude, an attitude of reverence, committed attention, and a deliberate commitment to work within a deeper dimension. We also realized that direct dialling was just that, dialling the number, and hi-fi was the focused state, our personal alertness which logged us on. The following are a series of writings given to us within the training period. They often threw us for a loop.

Dialling in – long-distance dialling – hi-fi on the move. Connections on alert – no barrier in dialling the distance. Two-dial link. Two-link connection – go ahead. Work on it, do the same – find frequency alone to tune in. Sounds great. Change tune regarding possibilities. Understand the changing demands.

Go further; we want the world to know our ability to cope with distant dialling – so far and so close. You will write a book. My lectures to you are for further filing. They will be coming forward sometime. You will hear a voice and juggle while listening. Stop!

Focus, focusing, maintaining balance. Do realize that larger scale is not obtained when small-scale equibalance is not achieved. Live as learned, growth through applications, set your view finder, and steady your hand – stand and focus.

Whatever place and time, you and your mates are not unlike right hand and left hand, each one functionally adapted to do their work. Together, though, they are able to undertake tasks otherwise impossible or very hard. Single-mindedness enables multiple tasks with success. Multifacetedness follows a range suitable for complex situations. A soul group brings this multifacetedness. When working together, a third dimension appears with added confidence and assuredness – the bloom on the flower, so to say.

149

When souls align, they become as one. Trust and co-operation work well in this atmosphere. A group of souls that align themselves start taking on a new form: A form all its own with its own dynamics. Part of the soul at large is in its astral form, part is here. Moments of trust and willingness allow it to combine within its fullest form. On ground level, when 'working out', it is sometimes difficult to find 'common ground'. When it is found, it is often very rewarding. Combined, it enables easier grounding and access to a higher level. The other group is always there.

Did you know that part of life is in you, and part of life is outside of you? A clue to our soul group participation is our continued effort to eliminate a sieve of critical thinking. This will elevate the language as well as clear thoughts. Put the thoughts out there and move on because dynamics are changing. Be crisp about things. Finish your work, clean up, and new platforms can take place.

In silence, one is not alone or lonely. The soul functions as a unit, as a centre. We are part and parcel of the great divine, the cog in the wheel. When asking for divine inspiration, ask for ultimate functioning and align oneself accordingly. The irony is that no one can do it alone, yet one has to trust that help is there regardless. And this is the lesson for each of us – help, listen, trust, and give. Emotionally and spiritually we will live in trust. As John Donne said, 'No man is an island'.

Follow your heart, dear one, for you know it will lead you where your soul should be.

Remember, remember, remember your circle of wholeness.
This circle is subject to external forces,
sometimes worse, sometimes less.
Your inner energy rebounds and rebirths
according to its vitality.
Sometimes you have to let go of some of all that is around.
Live the life and let the universe live its own.

Drawings as insight

Additional tools

In many ways working with this information was following the urgings of our heart. We have always felt that in doing this we were completing a karmic contract, and to do so has been a privilege.

As part of accessing of the soul and deeper thought, we always emphasized eliminating intrusions. We have talked about hypnosis, dream work, meditation, and regression as means to keep interference at bay. To this end we do require focus and quiet.

The other side of the coin is that thoughts are fleeting. We know about the dreams that fly away upon awakening. Thus, the drawings became like soul stenography. The jotting down of the deeper thought pattern bypasses the personal input. It was this doodling which expressed in simple shorthand a thought in black and white where round means wholeness, sides mean facets, and an arrow denotes direction. Reminders like these anchor where our thoughts have been.

Follow your heart, dear one!

The eyes – as windows of the soul

The drawings as such express themselves within the deeper meaning. We could call them writings without the words, using symbols to express things for which no words exist. This intuitive insight expresses the way a mandala might, helping us to access a deeper thought or subject.

In our reviewing, we came to see that the way the eyes were depicted in the automatic drawings was directly related to the apparent state of the person – alert, tired, overwhelmed, visionary, and so forth – on both the deeper and everyday aspects. Furthermore, we realized that the way the eyes had been depicted on individuals corresponded to the circles on the drawings that accompanied our more universal writings: microcosm to macrocosm or macrocosm to microcosm.

Some speak of the eyes as the window to the soul. We include this series of drawings of eyes for your contemplation.

151

Windows of the Soul

So little spoken,
So much said.
Muted masking of deeper feelings,
But oh – the eyes!

Chapter 14
Self-sourcing – meditation and mandalas

A picture is worth a thousand words

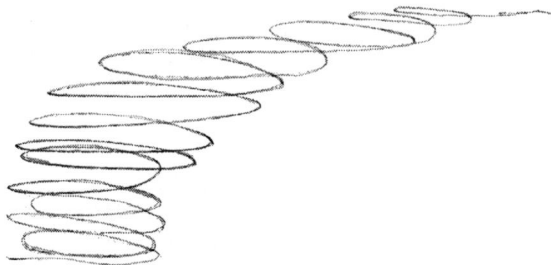

Self-sourcing: the why

This really is an application chapter, and as we progressed further in compiling the material into book form, we were constantly reminded not only to dialogue with our deeper Self, but to actually interact and dialogue with the Self. We had used the techniques and exercises repetitively over the years in our personal and professional lives so that they had become somewhat second nature, and it took us less time to gain access into our deeper selves. Breath was always an important gateway, and whenever we reached an impasse, we reverted to writing and drawings, our tried and true doorway to the team.

Self-sourcing is usually referred to as a way one dialogues with the Self. The overtone in these exercises is a meditative approach, which means in some way overriding the body and mind with their busy signals. These signals are silenced through actively quieting the body by means of a progressive relaxation, or by making use of the existing sleep state, as in dream work, self-hypnosis, and focusing on yogic movements.

Mind follows the same path of stilling through relaxation and breathing techniques, inducing a sleep state like meditation, during which the body and mind are at rest, although the mind stays alert. The mind can be occupied through activating senses using music, visual exercises, and engaging in creative work, which originates from a non-thinking place.

The integrating spirit writings have offered the body of thought behind our self-sourcing. Presently we offer you some of the avenues. The reason behind self-sourcing falls not only in the 'I want to know myself', but in the 'I want to know myself in a dimension that is outside the obvious reach of the Me'. Knowing oneself on the level of continuum in our eternal existence clearly offers insight into our purpose in this lifetime.

Recognition of soul mates in the different past relationships and recognition of inner potential, likes, and dislikes offer a vast view of the multidimensional Self. Although greatly subjective, we realize that interest focuses on areas that are of importance or simply wrangling within the self. Asking the why in the deepest and clearest dimension and footed by a non-judgemental attitude about what surrounds us, throws the ball into our own court. We leave you at it ...

Self-sourcing: stilling the mind – stilling the body – practice makes perfect

Interaction of body-mind and soul is derived through awareness of the mind and the subduing of the frequency of the body, our earthly vehicle. This is achieved through spiritual discipline. The exercises for mind and body are, in a certain sense, quite similar.

The mind must first stop and listen. The strenuous part is the discipline of meditation. Regularity and frequency both make the mind conquer strain and gain through achievement.

The body must first stop and listen. The strenuous part is the discipline of exercise.

These writings clearly state, 'Self-focusing requires motivation and dedication'. The rewards are a fuller understanding of yourself on your deeper levels and knowledge of your chosen soul purpose. The how? Stop and listen.

It is no accident that the drawing for meditation – sourcing the soul – is the same one as used for the soul itself.

Since time immemorial

For us it was imperative that we be in a meditative state in order to be able to access the team. Though this can be achieved in many different ways, we used a simple shift in focus. It is interesting to note what this writing points out: 'Since time immemorial' is used in order to enter into a contemplative frame of mind, and a deliberate shift must be made in either our movements, sounds, or focus. The trappings differ; the process is the same.

Meditation in its many forms has been part of our existence since time gone by. We find it back in the many cultures and religions, fitting within a belief system which finds value in capturing a state different from the 'everyday dealings' scenario. When looking for this quieter place, many of us automatically expresses ourselves in a manner focusing on quieting behaviour: rocking, humming, staring, and so forth. Religious groups might resort to kneeling, chanting, and focusing on religious items, such as stained glass windows or eliminating sights altogether by closing the eyes.

In Judaism, a rhythmic rocking will be utilized during prayers.

In Hinduism, these three elements of sound, posture, and visual focus are referred to as mantra, mudra, and mandala. They are called the three pillars of a platform and elevate us above the mundane in order to commune with the Self on a different and higher level. Often the meditation is paired with yogic exercises through which the physical is controlled in such a manner as to allow the mind to rise above it. Mandala as a physical focus reaches out to the busy and occupied mind to allow it to loosen from the grips of everyday interactions.

The Western world, with all its practicality, could understand advantages of meditation through its benefits in their search for promoting better health and stress combat. Scientific research into positive applications of meditative techniques found it lowered blood pressure, led to a better control of body functions, and changed brain patterns. This has brought further acceptance of meditation.

We would like to remind you to go a step further and look at the advantages on the deeper level. Because the soul is the infuser, one will be working with the self on its own turf to allow dialogue with the Self on the soul level. Meditation is the seclusion of the spirit from the body.

By any name and cultural incarnation, meditation has been the part of us that raised the thought to a mindless level of quiet.

Mantra – Mudra – Mandala

> *Sitting and sighing,*
> *breathing and dreaming,*
> *and let the Spirit rise.*

Exercise: setting the tone for meditation

There are many ways to set the tone for working in a meditative state: altering time, setting place, altering movement and activating the senses. When we began our work together we made use of all of the exercises given in this book doing them over and over again. Eventually with years of practice, and incorporating a meditative attitude into our thinking, entering this state of quiet and peacefulness became almost automatic. We could quickly clear the space, take a breath, refocus and we were there. Eventually our goal was to be able to walk in the world maintaining a meditative alertness. This is a goal we can sometimes achieve if we do not allow ourselves to be snagged in the drama of everyday events.

- **Time:** Being quiet, setting aside a regular time, acknowledging silence, awaiting responses.
- **Place:** Creating an area used only for meditation and quiet work – walking in Zen gardens, attending houses of worship, placing prayer rugs wherever you sit, wrapping yourself in special garments such as prayer shawls and blankets to shut out

the physical world, sitting in circle with respect for the other. This is really no different from our behaviour at times of special life events such as a wedding or funeral. We dress in a way that gives respect to the situation. This is a deliberate stepping away from our normal life and giving credence, by our clothes, to the special nature of the event.

- **Senses:** Using olfactory aids such as smudge and incense; changing movement patterns by kneeling, dancing, using rhythmic movements or assuming yogic positions; utilizing sound such as bells, repetitive sounds, chanting, and playing music. Making use of visual tools such as mental imagery and mandalas. All these ideas can also be powerful adjuncts to meditation and symbolize a temporary withdrawal from daily routine; they provide ways to create sacred space for focusing and quieting the mind, which is helpful in setting the stage for meditation.
- **Tone:** Before beginning your meditation, take a moment to set a tone of unconditional love and objectivity with a goal of attracting only that which will serve you. Give thanks to life and the life forms around you.
- **Recall:** Prior to doing your meditation, have available paper, pens, and paint. When you finish your meditation and before you speak, draw a mandala or write what has come to you from this universal source. Remain in the place of the observer and allow yourself to stand free from your own judgement or expectation. As closure, give thanks – a gesture of gratitude.

The following meditations vary in what may be seen as very subtle ways. One might speak more to a certain person than the other depending on whether that person's prime channel of functioning is the mind, the emotions, or the body.

Exercise: an unorthodox meditation

There is one line between two points, and it does not have to be a straight one. Allow it to roam and see why it curves a certain way. Watch it but stand back – many things have to go the way they have to. You are the observer, and like a mandala, the line leads you.

Now ... what insights do the shape or movement of the line bring you? Be precise! Take a step back and observe. Breathe deeply and let the quiet permeate you. Listen and listen deeply; look and look deeply. Unfocus your eyes, unfocus your hearing, unfocus your thinking, and infuse yourself with love. Then translate any questions that emerge into everyday terms, but permeate your questioning with love.

Exercise: meditation – body-mind-soul

1. Seat yourself comfortably; close your eyes.
2. Feel your body supported by your chair, the floor, and the air around it.
3. Feel yourself completely present.
4. Notice your breath; follow its rhythm as you inhale and exhale.
5. Let its rhythm clear the mind and its thoughts – follow it like a wave of water washing away any unnecessary debris.
6. Allow yourself to sink into a place of relaxed alertness with no agenda other than following your breath.
7. As you feel yourself sinking deeper and deeper into the nothingness, see what catches your attention. Observe it and gently let it go.
8. Return to your place of attentiveness and once again sink deeper and deeper into the nothingness
9. Repeat until the mind and body dissolve into the nothingness.

A brief word on breath

When referring to breathing throughout this section on application, we are speaking of the yogic form: inhaling through the nose and exhaling through the mouth. The abdomen distends on the inhale and collapses inward on the exhale, eventually falling into a rhythmic loop, where the inhalations and exhalations become as one. It takes some practice to master this method, but to do so is well worth the effort, because it is the basis of all meditative and self-sourcing techniques. Breath is referred to in many of the writings as prana, the earth energy; it is both our essence and our primordial aspects in one. Breath brings us back to our first moments of life and is often the final visual clue when we exit this earthly plane.

Mantras

Mantra is achieved through sound, incantations, and sacred sayings. The aim is to align and merge oneself and one's vibration with a clearer one. Sounding sacred words, like 'aum' and 'amen', submits one to another frequency. Not unlike the tuning of an instrument to the proper note, it is becoming one within the concert of the universe – just as Mozart said he did not compose the music but rather went to this other place from where he wrote down whatever he heard.

Just as group meditation is used to support one another to change the vibration of a larger whole, so it is with group chanting. Thus we become a part of a whole and not only the drummer who marches to his own tune.

How interesting that in this writing the arrow is used as an example of a symbol. It refers to the simplicity and yet power of symbol which exists outside of the verbal. Much misunderstanding and subsequent discord arose around the treaty rights of the First Nations people of the Americas. Their tradition existed outside of writing, and yet their agreements and treaties were woven into the design of their wampum belts, an example of cultural transmission. For them this was undisputedly a contract; for the Europeans not. Like our drawings, symbols and renderings can be subjective.

Mudra, mantra, and mandala are three traditional Buddhist methods of self-sourcing. Mudra is position, mantra is sound, and mandala is visual. All three are tools for focusing and centring in the now, aligning one's body, mind, and spirit with its deepest calling. They can be described as the three pillars of a platform on which the spirit rests.

Today many of these practices have been extrapolated from Buddhism into a myriad of forms, religious and spiritual alike. In fact, throughout history many peoples, religions, and practices have utilized sound, position, and drawing for spiritual alignment and healings, such as drumming, tribal dancing, and sand paintings.

Mudra is a gesture or posture, like tai chi, a concentration on movement which becomes a ritual. Or it can be sustained positions like the asanas in yoga. Yoga can be done purely for strengthening and flexibility. However, when applied as a spiritual practice, it can be a gateway to freedom from our daily trappings and bodily demands. In extreme cases, as lived by the yogis in concert with denial and austerity, it can lead one into the realm of asceticism.

Mantra is a combination of sacred symbols that forms a nucleus of spiritual energy. This serves as a magnet to attract or a lens to focus spiritual vibrations. The root 'mano' in Sanskrit means 'to think'; 'tra' comes from 'trai', meaning to protect from the bondage of the phenomenal world. Therefore, mantra means the thought that liberates and protects. Its power is felt to increase through the repetition of sounds – for example, 'aum'. Mantra silences the active mind through repetitive sound. Popular today is the kirtans, a call-and-response chant genre that uses ancient Sanskrit mantras. It is not dissimilar to Gregorian chants and other church-based chanting.

Mandala is an expression or form, again coming from Sanskrit. 'Mano' means mind and 'dala' means expansion or unfoldment; 'dala' also means a device or tool that evokes an expansion of consciousness. Through the use of a mandala, the mind can increase its content or range.

All three require deliberateness in our actions in order to be able to move beyond our physical surroundings. Mudra requires that we move through bodily discomforts until we reach a place where the body can submit to our will and rise above its immediate demands to a greater spiritual place. Mantra silences the sometimes constant chatter of the thinking mind through repetitive sound, aligning us and our vibration to a place of merger with a clearer sound, a place where we are in tune with the constant of the universe. Mandala requires us to bypass the logical mind and let form emerge from the formless place of feeling, the seat of our deepest creativity.

Since ancient times, man and woman have expressed themselves in symbols, lines, dots, and figures, telling where they were going, what they were hunting, and what was important in life. These visual depictions were one of the ways culture was transmitted. As time progressed, many of these symbols became the basis of letters used in our present-day writing. A combination of these letters became words and a way of creatively expressing ourselves.

Nevertheless, lines, arrows, dots, colours, and shapes maintained a place which were neatly their own, expressing thoughts without words.

We are repeatedly reminded about the importance of drawings. In essence, all our writings in the book have a mandala footprint underlay. Thus we were made made aware that we are visually wired and express ourselves this way. These visual renderings also solidify our thought, like an architect's drawings detailing the planning stages of the work.

When thoughts are trailing, written symbols focus on specifics – the directions of mullings – punctuating emotional highlights in the meantime and ignoring rules of penmanship or artistic endeavour. We are allowed to hold onto a track on which our mind travelled. In essence, all our writings have a mandalic underlay.

Mnemonics, the art of memory, goes a step further by use of the visual approach. The way prayer beads keep track of a sequence of prayers, a mandala keeps the thought pattern in a manner that offers guidance to the quiet Self. It frees the thought to flow without having to be reminded of time and order. While speaking to you, you enable those thoughts to anchor themselves and save them from getting lost. A speaker might use the map of a garden to remind him where his speech takes a turn or where a highlight is in the topic being discussed. Dream work and retrieval of dreams greatly benefits from teaching oneself to capture these thoughts.

Mandala, in essence, frees the physical from grounding the self. Deeply intricate, winding, bending, and connecting lines can be visually followed in a way that allows the physical to free itself and to leave the deeper personal aspect to roam. We encourage working with self-expression through drawing work. We enclose the little drawings in the book on purpose and as an example, knowing very well that these mandala drawings are very individual expressions of a deeper thought. We might add that they are sublime in simplicity, yet they are also storytelling. We are now back to square one, where an arrow meant 'this is going there to do that'.

We essentially grab a concept in a form that does not need wording, but often we find that having accomplished this, we might retrieve our deeper thoughts, giving them a belated verbal expression.

Conduit

Fed from an unknown source,
Meditation locks out the everyday.
Pictures appear,
Inspiration for the artist's breath.
I paint with the stroke of words.

Utilizing mandalas: a talk with the self

The essence of focusing into mandala work enables us to step outside the self and touch base with the tremendous capacity to transgress borders of thought and enter the source of feeling.

Exercise: creating a mandala

In order to access one's uncharted corners through mandala, the notion that one cannot draw has no place. In preparation, one must remove all critical thinking. Given our propensity for self-criticism, we must be vigilant about staying outside the bounds of 'how things should look'. A few minutes of regular, daily exercise will show a changing outlook and pattern in this regard.

Just as the Rorschach is a blob subject to any interpretation, it is, in essence, the door to a particular thought which was standing in front of the mind, awaiting expression.

With mandala drawing, the thoughts come forward unhindered. Symbols, colours, shapes, and narrative are a part of the process, just like in dream work, where retrieval of a dream must occur as quickly as possible. So with mandala, scribing the words, which describe the drawing, should be done immediately upon its completion. We have to remember that mandala is an abstract expression for non-figurative thinking. Hence the drawing can be a Garden of Eden, or a lightning bolt with a blob on top of it.

Preparation for the creation of a mandala follows the process for clearing one's mind, described in this chapter in 'Setting the tone for meditation'. Have drawing materials at hand. Following the process of quieting and clearing the mind, and then let your doodling begin. Without judgement about the outcome, review your drawing and the descriptive words that emerged.

Anecdotal writing

Here is advice given in a meditation on the personal preparation needed to assist others in the opening of their deeper seeing, the third eye.

In wiping the sleep
from the eyes of those
who are awakening,
you must first wipe the
sleep from your own.

Dream work

Waking time is one's lucid time: The body is still in its sleeping mode, and the mind is rested but waking up and not yet bombarded by the daily throws. When mind the driver is at rest, it hashes and rehashes the routes it took. In its still right-brain mode, where thoughts are abstract and conversations are encoding in symbolism, it deals with events at hand, evaluates the problems, and looks for answers. It checks events, touches on the unsaid and hidden thoughts, and finds the snippets so carefully kept out of reach when alert.

We can train ourselves to access the rich realms of dreamtime. Writing your awakening thoughts can teach you to reach your dreams and take them out before your awareness closes them down. When the regression reaches down to far, far away, your soul, your dream work, talks to your spirit.

Dreams

Notes from the unconscious,
Unopened letters to yourself:
A treasure trove – a gold mine – a dialogue on the sly.

PSST!

They say mosquito nets
are for keeping out bugs.
I know better;
they are royal weavings
for keeping in dreams.

Exercise: dream retrieval

1. To begin, keep a pencil and pad of paper close by your bed; recall most often occurs in the first moments of wakefulness. Jotting your dreams down guards against the possibility of forgetting exact details as the flood of daily activities ensues. Recording also allows for review of the information at a later date. This can be particularly important if your dreams are prophetic in nature. Trusting the accuracy of your dream-given information may sharpen your ability to notice the many symbols and clues from your everyday surroundings. Dreams are another way of sourcing unconscious information during waking hours.
2. Set the tone and conditions for recall before bedtime. Try to relax before dropping off to sleep. You can do a progressive relaxation to accomplish this (see the section on the body).
3. Give your unconscious mind the instruction to remember the significant images of your dreamtime.
4. It can also be important to notice whether you have recurrent images in your dreams; for example, you always see yourself in flight. If in fact your life is spent predominantly in an anchored mode, and in your dreams you often take flight, perhaps the part of you that is ready to fly is asking you to try something new.

5. Though you may consult one who works with dreams, what your dreams mean to you is the most important factor. The possibilities for interpretation are limitless. Your dreams can be the gateway to realms unimagined and unexplored.

Retrieval

Grains of remembrance
Slipping through the cracks of my consciousness.
Thin threads
To be rewoven into the texture of my dreams.

Irretrievable

I do not welcome waking,
Hesitant to leave the dream world,
Reluctant to face the reality of day.
I am fearful
The images and symbols of my dreams,
So clear, so precious,
Will fade.

Regression

Regression is yet another means of self-sourcing, but one that comes with many caveats; it's not for beginners. We will reach a point where we are pulled, even compelled to know more. When this happens, past life regression is to be used in relation to this life and its relevance – hence the warning, 'Don't get caught in storytelling'. We are reminded that when utilizing regression, be specific in the questioning. To this we would add, work with a person not only well-trained in regressive techniques but who has an understanding of one's emotional and psychological needs. At once effective and powerful in accessing and releasing past events that have held the person in a grip of unpleasant memory, what is unearthed through regression can also be extremely upsetting. Regression will also sometimes occur spontaneously through familiarity with place, smells, sights, or sounds, depending on one's particular sensitivities. This is especially common in children up to the age of four. A feeling of déjà vu can occur with people whom you are certain you have known before. You likely have. Seeing people in their present-day situation is essential in giving a functional context to the experience. Recalling more glamorous lives and people can also be a way of snagging us into unreal expectations. It is essential that the relevance of the information accessed through regression be grounded in one's present-day life – 'What is the learning for this life?' is the key rationale for using regression. This last point raises the issue of karma. Unfinished business from another existence may surface in a regression, begging to be resolved. This is using regression to link with our deeper goals. It serves us well to remember that regression is reality on a different level.

Our soul is the transitory and reminiscing vehicle. In the search of Self, there comes a time when the need to meet the soul on its own turf becomes a haunting wish. Snippets of information, having entered our minds without the grounds of being there, become part of the search for answers to the 'who' that we really are. Déjà vu, unexplained talents, likes and dislikes, and unanswered reasons for feeling closeness to certain places or persons are leads to be followed.

Often facilitated by someone who is capable of guiding us to unknown places, one sets out in search of the Self. In the deepest reverence to the space around us, the deepest meditative state is being reached. It is helpful to prepare oneself with the precise wording of one's goal. For many, a prayer will set the tone for the sanctity of the endeavour. Though this type of search would not necessarily be a beginner's project, it is within anyone's reach according to Edgar Cayce in The Sleeping Prophet. *He maintains that anyone could learn to do what he did if only they applied themselves!*

Applying oneself is not a mean feat if one goes over all the meditative writings again. Consider looking for life's purpose and ask your questions such as:

1. Where was I?
2. What is the reason why the life in which I look now is important to my present one?

3. Who were the people I lived with, and why were they important to me?
4. What did I learn from that specific life, and what am I to learn now?
5. What is my soul purpose, and why am I important to people in my present life?

But may we end by telling you that life is to be lived in the present. This life is your learning. This life is the one that counts. On the soul level one knows its purpose.

Regression is like looking in an old photo album – people are gone, places have changed, all became past.

The Potter

Leprechaun or alchemist,
High priest or Maccabee,
Once again we meet.
Not on battlefields of England,
Nor on Mediterranean shores,
But here in this Ontario forest.
We commune under pines planted by hand
In the presence of your ceramic green frog,
Watchful guardian of the pond.
Once you fashioned pots in the desert;
Today you skilfully ply your trade
Shaping clay for eager tourists.
As they sip tea from your earthen cups,
Do they feel the magic?

Chapter 15
Self-sourcing:
senses and chakras

Our connectors

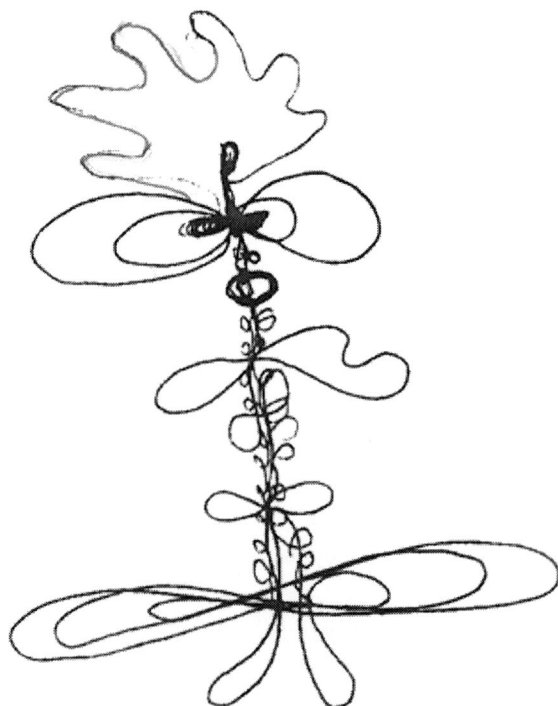

As we proceeded further into these application chapters, we found it interesting that the team made a point of addressing the senses and chakras as separate components within these self-sourcing application writings. We were reminded that both the senses and chakras are gateways through which we as entities can interact with our surroundings.

A brief aside: Looking back we realize that we were both intuitive and that this intuition and our awareness were in a heightened mode. These discoveries prompted us to be curious, and so we were drawn to a variety of practices and studies that sharpened and enhanced our understanding of the functions and usefulness of our chakras and senses. Always we were questioning what we were learning and applying the knowledge in our private and professional lives, our working laboratory. However, though our physical senses serve to make us aware of our surroundings, the chakras in contrast have the ability to connect us with our deeper selves. We realized that in this chapter we were being given an expanded application of the material, one that had quite a different slant. Once again we were being jostled out of complacency and habitual thinking. Let's let the writings speak for themselves.

The senses

Perhaps the essence of this writing on the senses and their various manifestations is the Greek adage, 'Everything in moderation', for even too much of a good thing can take us farther away from our goal of spiritual fulfilment. Hearkening back to a former writing, *'Drop one, gain one; drop a physical need, gain a spiritual one'.*

The physical must first have had its needs sated; only then can we move to the richness of contentment available on the soul level. One could hear this as a subtle warning which harkens back to the oft-repeated and central tenet of all the writings: we are the drivers of our own growth, and balance is what we are striving to achieve. We offer the following exercises as an introduction to enhancing the senses through nature and experiencing your own energy or astral field.

Regarding the vehicle notion of oneself, we would like to discuss the senses and chakras. What are they, what are they doing, and how do we utilize this knowledge? From a physical point of view, one can find out and know exactly what they do. They make you hear, see, feel, smell, and taste. It is hard to ignore their input because they are vital for one's well-being and interaction with the world.

From the soul level, both the senses and the chakras are regarded as the instrumentation of the total vehicle. On the physical level they function automatically; we can set the dials and they can interact. This is not the case on the soul level. Here the senses and chakras mainly work as intermediaries between the physical body and the auric body.

We do not stop where our visual physical ends; rather our energy field (called our astral field or aura) extends itself around us and is influenced by our body. On our astral level or soul base, we do have these connective counterparts as well. The senses work and interact on the physical and sensing level. The senses also enhance the astral or soul-based level through corresponding stimulation and increased vibration. Senses can elevate or depress the I-they-us. Enriching the self through sound, sight, taste, and touch increases happiness, enhances vibration, and raises the soul.

Surround yourself with pleasant interactions and sights. Aromatherapies, laughter tapes, sound and colour, simple foods, and appreciation of all enhances the function of the self. The opposite side of the coin is that overabundance is to the detriment of the sensitive tool and causes the dulling of the instrument, which subsequently will need increased stimulation.

Throughout these writings we focus on our vehicle, our mechanical notion, but we do hope to get the analogy across. In essence, our physical senses interact with our surroundings and enrich our daily life, bringing the fullness to our earthly existence. On the soul level the enrichment brings us to a state of contentment, having saturated the physical needs and allowing us an increased vibrational level. This supplants the daily needs level to a plane of spiritual fulfilment. The hierarchy of needs is then met.

Exercise: utilizing nature

Nature invites us to discover her many offerings, to attune to her moods and rhythms, and to notice all that surrounds us.

With an increased awareness of the importance of physical fitness, many of us already find ourselves out in nature much more than ever. However that time is often spent engaging in various and sundry activities: walking, fishing, golfing, bird watching, or playing tennis, all of which are valuable for physical and mental balance. Yet there are other ways of being in communion with the natural environment, ways that can put us in touch with our internal environment. Often we happen upon them by accident. Ask runners about the natural high or state they find themselves in after a long run. How then can we tap into that rhythm or space deliberately? What tools does nature offer to facilitate that process? Our five senses are our best toolkit for adding deliberateness to our everyday activities. While walking in the woods, you can invite the participation of all of your senses to be there in heightened awareness.

- **Sight:** As you walk, notice the various aspects of nature – the beauty, the colours, the shapes. How do the different seasons look to you?
- **Taste:** Walk further; are there fruits or plants you can pick and savour?
- **Touch:** Stop and take time to lie on the ground and feel yourself become one with the earth as it touches your body; realize the wholeness of your relationship to the earth and all that it provides.
- **Smell:** Allow yourself to smell the ground itself or the plants; what does this stir in you? Do any memories of past times arise?
- **Sound:** Listen fully to all of the sounds – the birds, the wind as it rustles the leaves, the water passing over rocks, the animals scampering. Take note of your own breath within it all.

To hone our spiritual selves, a focus and commitment must be present.

To look – to taste – to listen – to touch – to smell.

1. Equip yourself with a journal or notepad and pen.
2. Set aside a weeklong period and commit to noting how you relate to nature on a daily basis.
3. Upon waking, notice the weather – is it sunny, rainy, warm, cool? What bearing if any does that have on your mood?
4. As you proceed with your day, take time to witness nature: take a walk, watch the clouds, smell the smells, and allow the sounds of nature to permeate you, taking time again to notice what specific effects these conditions have upon you.
5. At day's end, take time for a walk to review the events of the day. Allow the positive events of the day to fill your system and

empower you. Let the negative events slide out of your person and into the ground.

6. Imagine you are filling your system with the regenerative energy of the earth.

7. At the end of the week, review your notes and take stock. What particular places or conditions of nature energize you? What, if anything, depletes you?

8. Have you allotted yourself the amount of unwinding time you need to consort with nature?

Hopefully the answer is yes, and in so doing, I became more aware. I took the wheel and became the driver of my own vehicle. I claimed my day, I claimed the world around me, and I claimed myself.

Creativity

With the heightened awareness of our senses and feelings, we enter into a new relationship with ourselves. From this place of awareness our creativity can flow naturally. Creativity is the outward expression of our soul life. Having said that, we would be remiss if we did not make the link between creativity and the senses, for the senses are the realms within which the muses dwell. We refer you back to chapters three and four, which deal with integrating spirit and being all you can. Within those chapters, the beautiful writing 'Free Spirit' offers a poetic description of the creativity-soul partnership. Poems have the ability to elicit strong responses. In 'Elemental' nature stirs the emotions, whereas in 'Moonstruck' nature is an energizer. You may wish to make a journal or notepad your constant companion to capture those creative insights as they occur, because the spontaneous is just that: there when it chooses, inattentive to our timetables.

The following poems and 'Moonstruck', the final poem of the chapter, reflect the polar responses which nature, given her power and diversity, is able to evoke.

Elemental

Yesterday, swept away by wind, and churning water,
Turbulence and desperation met within.
Today I sit in quiet contemplation,
The ocean a soft presence.

Frustration

Silly brain,
Where are you when I need you
To conjure up a word?
When I flop into bed,
Weary, begging for sleep,
You present a multitude of metaphors.
Untamed mass of grey cells!

Chakras

Chakras give another vantage point from which to look at the body and its higher energy and spiritual function. Our chakras are the energy centres aligned along the spine, from the base of the spine to a place above the skull. It is thought these centres have an astral, corresponding form that surrounds our physical form, and these chakras correspond with our outside energy field.

Many cultures recognize energy channels throughout the body. Chinese medicine acknowledges the chakras as energy points but uses meridians, the lines through which energy is transmitted throughout the body, in the delivery of acupuncture. Reflexology also utilizes energy points: practitioners manipulate the nerve endings in the foot, addressing these pathways of energy direction and flow.

Until recently, the Western world has rarely worked with chakras and their potential. Western civilization, being very energetic, like to think strength and vigour can overcome all notions of personal weakness through sheer willpower. Self-expression is often seen as a sign of weakness. Introspectives are sometimes called 'navel gazers'.

The body has seven chakras: root, belly, solar plexus, heart, throat, brow (third eye), and crown. Above the crown, the interpersonal chakra, sometimes called the interpersonal-soul chakra, is shared by both our physical and our astral body. The implication of its function goes very deep – or better said, very high. Chakra levels are often assigned sensory meanings through colour, sound, and visualization. In sound, it is generally accepted that base sounds represent the lower chakras, with higher sounds represented in the ascending chakras. The 'aum' or 'amen', the white sound, encompasses the whole energy field.

Do not forget the vehicle notion of the body: the soul is the passenger and the driver; it will be there.

Keeping the chakras balanced requires discipline and commitment. Regularity and frequency will greatly enhance the functionality of the instrumentation and the relay of energy.

Again the silence is in directed sound. Clarity is in directed visualization.

Exercise: rainbow meditation

This is an effective meditation using the senses to energize the chakras and to reinforce the connection between the senses and chakras, through sound and visualization. Follow the basic steps for meditation as outlined in the previous chapter. In this meditation each chakra has a corresponding note and colour. Familiarize yourself with them as listed below before beginning your meditation.

Root Chakra:	Location: base of the spine; colour: red; note: *do;* drone on sound: *ooo*
Belly:	Location: in the belly; colour: orange; note: *re;* drone on sound: *oh*
Solar Plexus:	Location: above the navel, below the breast; colour: yellow; note: *mi;* drone on sound: *aw*
Heart:	Location: across the chest in the area of the heart; colour: green; note: *fah;* drone on sound: *ah*
Throat:	Location: at the throat; colour: sky blue; note: *sol;* drone on sound: *eh*
Brow:	Location: between the eyebrows, seat of the third eye; colour: midnight blue, indigo; note: *lah;* drone on sound: *lh*
Crown:	Located five or six inches above the head; colour violet; note *ti* – drone on sound *eee*
All Chakras (The Interpersonal):	Visualize all simultaneously; colour: white; note: moves from low *do* to high *do;* droning sound: *ohm*

Variation 1
Close your eyes and focus your attention on a chakra, beginning first with the root and moving one at a time through all of them to the

crown. Visualize the colour associated with the chakra while intoning the associated sound. Bring the colour through your feet and up to the base of the chakra, let the colour swirl in the shape of a figure eight, and then allow the to colour spiral up through the body to the top of the head until it spouts out through the top of your head like a fountain and flows down and into the earth again. Repeat with the next chakra.

This sounding pattern establishes a quiet connection within yourself and your body.

Variation 2

A second sounding pattern used in Kundalini practice functions as an awakening of the chakras. Once again, ascending from the root to the crown, the sound is chanted repeatedly as one focuses on the chakra.

Sounds: root 'lam', belly 'vam', solar plexus 'ram', heart 'yam' or 'yum', throat 'hum', brow 'ohm', crown 'silent'.

Variation 3

Let the music lead you; follow the notes of the music you are hearing and notice in which chakra the music. The music of Paganini or flute selections from Zamfir in the background will support the higher chakras, Chopin supports the middle, and Mozart and Gregorian or Tibetan chants the lower. You may also experiment with music of your own to feel the difference.

Sound is a powerful tool, both positive and negative; it can strengthen or deplete. For further explorations into the effect of music on the physical body, we recommend: *The Healing Energies of Music* by Hal Lingerman and Kay Gardner's CD *A Rainbow Path*.

Energy work: a bridge

The bridge into the mainstream using energy work has been built in Western culture through therapeutic touch, which was systematized by Dolores Krieger, former nursing director of New York Hospital. Krieger trained nurses to work with the electromagnetic field around the body – our aura. Initially, she and her nurses were known as

'Krieger's Crazies' (Gerber, 2002), but the results they produced were effective and measurable. By reinforcing the energy field of the patient's body, they literally gave it a boost of energy, which emanated from the hands of the practitioners. The nurses were able to induce states of calm, decrease pain, and promote speedier healing.

The following is an insightful writing explaining therapeutic touch and its benefits. It treats therapeutic touch, a generic term similar to Kleenex, as another application of energy usage.

Therapeutic touch in all its names

Such a lovely name, so many forms it takes, and so many ways to express itself. Every astral level is the expression of the physical self it encapsulates. One functions with the other in conjunction; one mirrors the other. One-oneself is the double-edged sword with which we ramble.

In the physical entity, the electrical field of our millions of cells is combined into an energy form that gives us the impetus to function as a whole. Disruption into the energy field for many reasons creates a disturbance, interruption, or overtriggering of specific areas within this physical field, which increases interrupted circuits in other areas.

Chi, prana, energy – it is there, it is measurable, and it is palpable. Our physical does not stop where our visual does. We extend beyond ourselves and function with and within this form. Visualization directs itself from the inside out and demands support for the physical on the ethereal level in order to redirect the physical course of a life event. The therapeutic intervention is the quest and request to have the energy level re-established on the astral level of our astral body as a way to re-enhance the physical depletion and encourage healing on the physical level.

Redirection of energy is done in many ways and forms. Energy direction, massages, and therapeutic touch are some of the forms. Energy direction restores energy circulation internally. Massages and hatha forms revitalize functioning of the physical. Actively and passively, therapeutic touch is the non-manipulative, astral-directed energy enabler.

Visualization works from the mind and inside out; therapeutic touch works from outside in. In conjunction, the two complement each other and should be used bi-conditionally.

Energy forms to be used:

177

Chi: The energy forms of all living things – trees, nature, all things viable. Enjoy them, stand close to them, and use visualization to bi-condition with clarity.

Prana: Use the planet's energy form through breathing exercises – see it come, see it go, and watch its gentle effects.

People: Love them all and enjoy their dynamic, there is great strength in being in positive relationships with our social part and partners; large, common-minded groups have an exponential strength form.

More on energy: visible proof

The energetic part of our being goes by many names: aura, electromagnetic field, and astral. Mention of its names and a suggestion that it is concrete and palpable is still a topic of controversy. Therefore, a note of thanks is due the Kirlians for establishing visible proof of its existence (Brugh, 1979). This Russian couple developed a technique for photographing our energetic field. Using a metal plate, they were able to capture these emanations on film. Named after them, Kirlian photography has been in existence since the 1940s.

Exercise: discovering your energy field

Rub your hands together several times as you would when trying to warm up. Then, spread your hands apart a foot or two from one another, moving them ever so slightly in and out. Gradually bring your hands towards one another in an inward motion; continue to do so until you find a place where it feels as though something is pushing your hands apart. It may have a feeling similar to the stretching of an elastic band. That place of resistance is the perimeter of your electro-magnetic field. To locate it, you will have to be attentive to the very subtle quality of energetic emanations. However, if you wish to use your hands for scanning, such sensitivity will be a necessary ally.

Energy work expanded

We mentioned astral scanning briefly, having dealt more thoroughly with one form of energy usage, therapeutic touch. Yet how can we ignore astral scanning when we have mentioned its many forms so often? Scanning the astral is the diagnostic tool of those who work with hands off the body. With hands held three to four inches from the skin, practitioners move their hands along the energy field of their client to detect areas of excess or depletion. Once found, they either boost or draw off the energy as needed; the practitioner either provides additional energy or draws it off. Therapeutic touch has formalized scanning into a specific format and sequence.

In Conclusion

We take leave of this chapter, recognizing that much more could be said about the senses and chakras, because the areas they span are vast and richly textured. With the many disciplines, which use it as a routine foundation, energy work alone could be reviewed in – depth, but to do so, we would have to fill another book and perhaps will. To learn to work with the subtlety of energy is the subject of many workshops. The senses and their impact can be a journey into the creative arts and their relationship to healing – still more to write and to teach. However, for purposes of this book, consider this section a sampling, one that we hope will entice you to explore the rich number of choices available.

Moonstruck

*Full bodied moon
Cast upon the water,
Your essence shimmers earthward.*

*Clouds open to receive your sensuality,
Wild winds dance the leaves,
Skies respond with pink electricity.*

*Nature intensifies;
My body pulses*

In rhythmic harmony.
Bed beckons.

Riveted, seduced,
How can I leave?

Chapter 16
The human condition: windows on the world

Meeting life's challenges soulfully

We have divided this chapter into several areas, utilizing a fair number of personal consultations. This inclusion was deliberate, because these 'windows on the world' reflect the problems people encountered as they engaged in their daily routines. All of the personal anecdotal writings presented in the book were provided for clients in our clinic. Bogged down with issues and worries, they asked for advice. The writings are the answers given to us by the team. We thank our clients for allowing us to publish some of these writing. Because of their universality, we wished to share them. Often the answers provided were focused on issues that were lying on a much deeper level; this depth in turn elicited a deep response that was always surprisingly on target.

Though the thread of connection between topics may seem a silken one, they are all linked by the theme of living and embracing life in the present – for it is these situations, with their ever-changing joy and turmoil, which keep us anchored to the physical.

We have also included some exercises. Some of the topics dealt with are belief, goal setting, fear, disruption, distraction, loss, and love.

Consolidation: introductory narrative

John Lennon and Yoko Ono, in their song 'Beautiful Boy', wrote, 'Life is what happens when you're busy making other plans', which accurately describes our experience as we immersed ourselves in the onerous task of bringing this book to completion.

In the preface we spoke of having found ourselves in a place of discomfort when our connection to our teaching team first came about. How, we wondered, could we ever integrate our experiences into our everyday life? Now as we began writing what we thought would be the final chapter of this book, we were once again dislodged from our place of comfort. 'The human condition', a chapter dedicated to unravelling the same old dilemmas of adjustment, confronted us with a multitude of chaotic and confusing thoughts.

We come to you with a greater appreciation of the fact that we all have to deal with the roadblocks we encounter, though we may not do so with the elegance to which we would aspire. The fact that we had the benefit of our teachings behind us did not exempt us from the challenges of everyday reality. Though we could understand and appreciate the reasons behind what had happened, we would react to the setbacks with the same degree of frustration as anyone else. Perhaps what our background has brought to us is a shorter recovery time.

We have named this portion 'Consolidation' because we recognized, through having undergone our own external glitches, that we are changing beings asked to cope with an ever-changing environment. Because those changes take many forms, we too are required to adapt in many ways. It forced us to look at the messages of this book's teachings in a very practical, grounded, mundane, everyday way. How, we asked ourselves, can this deeper wisdom and the insights contained in this book guide us through these tough times? See chapter nine, 'To learn is to grow'. The 'Dada of doing things' in that particular chapter admonished us to be flexible, be aware of the world around us, and be creative in order to be better prepared for the ever changing dynamics of life.

This approach invites us to look critically at ourselves and to ask: Are we living from a position of strength? Are we operating to our fullest potential? Is what we value internally being lived externally? Or are we living within a mode that we have outgrown? If so, are we willing to change to a new mode? All of which is asking us, have we committed to living a life infused by soul?

As we address the issue of living the human condition in this context, we do so with great compassion, knowing that we are going to attract all kinds of situations, of greater and lesser discomfort. We realize that these bumps along the way actually encourage this soulful course of action, and so as we look critically at ourselves, let that gaze be one of acceptance and understanding. A gentle approach with one's self, along with a large dose of curiosity and attentiveness, can work wonders in easing the challenges we encounter.

Early on in our studies, the team, acknowledging how different the two of us are, referred to us as the right hand and left hand. These differences have served us well, extending our potential as we explored the depth of the material. Always our responses were so different, and that uniqueness made for many a lively discussion. Like sampling food from different cultures, it enriched both of us, and we are grateful for the miracles of aliveness it has added to our lives. There is no doubt we will miss our writing sessions because writing this book has allowed us to explore the deeper meaning of our lives, taking us far below the surface. However, at the same time we are eager to share the material and look forward to meeting our readership in teaching forums and dialogues.

All is one

The following is a perfect writing to set the tone for an attitude of open-heartedness towards life and one's own limitations.

This chapter is anchoring the feet to the ground, so to speak. Remove any misconceptions that the element that is called spirit lives in a domain separate from that which we call the material. Both move and mesh in the ethers like smoke dissipating through the air. They are to be lived and breathed as one, two parts of an exquisite whole. So in this chapter, we confront birth and death, love and frustration, and how we set our course, as aspects of an inseparable whole.

Anecdotal writing: transitioning

This personal writing dealing with death was given to a forty-year-old woman, who questioned the imminent death of her mother. The daughter was not coping well with her mother's pending passage and requested the writing. What this approach did was remind her of her link to the universal dimension and the concept that death is a part of living – not the regular form of consolation, but it very much bolstered her.

Give time to dignity,
Give time to loving,
Give time to dying,
Because it is you that is perpetuated;
all of the time we have to stand still
and listen to ourselves
is the time which our whole existence is built upon.
What we love and feel in our self
is what our whole essence is about.
The moments we deny ourselves
to think and
talk to ourselves
will be gone
and never retrieved.
This is our moment of dealing with eternity
as it is given.
Each turn of events is left to destiny,
and reflection upon it
is what makes us whole.

In this instance, loving has to do with acceptance of the process of withdrawal from the physical plane and the love, which can be lived within these cycles of completion. It counsels us on the importance of taking time for quiet reflection. Here we could consider the team's discussion on soul: *'interaction with the silent Self is the basis for true self-reliance'*. The writing also reassures both mother and daughter of the perpetuation of the person through the continuity of the soul and its timeless nature.

The next writing leads us into the realm of loving life and carefully selecting our life choices.

Love's implications

This personal writing was given to us when we were still uncertain as to the course the book would take. One way of looking at this writing is to see it was telling us how to clear time and space for writing without guilt – a move of trust that our lives would not fall apart, that our family obligations would not go by the wayside. If read closely, the team is telling us to set our priorities and go for it! You'll know it's right because it will feel pleasurable. Understanding the implications of love is knowing when bondage ends and duty takes over. Sense of duty is self-implied. You have to realize that the difference between loving, doing, and duty is the implication one's self puts on it. Let your love have more of a chance. You cannot take in all; be selective, look for priorities, and please love them. There is no karmic let-down if you are not perfect. Working hard is already ribbon burning. You will know it is the divine order because you will be doing what you love.

Artful

*I am eating too much
and writing too little.
Shepherding a flock
that no longer needs tending.
I pour my creativity
into a house that already*

> *brims with the artful,*
> *Cooking meals devoid of ingenuity,*
> *Fearing that my epitaph will read,*
> *'Famous for her chicken'.*

It is appropriate to revisit the theme of consolidation, because this poem speaks of times when we find ourselves spiralling back into old patterns of behaviour, done out of obligation – or living within a mode which we have created but have outgrown. These old patterns may not fit anymore, but the new ones may not necessarily be in place yet. Herein lays the challenge: How to change those habitual ways? How to weather through the potential confusion and chaos of these times as we attempt to re-align with our deeper Self? To do so requires trust, curiosity, flexibility, and an ability to be vulnerable.

Given that the dynamics of life are always in a state of mobility and flux, two often discomfort-inducing states, do we delude ourselves into thinking that we are in a static place? Perhaps we do because things which are fixed can appear to be more stable. Yet the opposite is the case – it is the place of rigidity, which is more vulnerable, and the place of flexibility, which is stronger. Consider the willow in the windstorm, able to flex and bend. Or the softshell crab, who has shed its crusty covering and is considered by epicures more precious when in this vulnerable state.

In many ways, this writing incorporates the messages of the two that have gone before: love yourself and don't get caught up in obligations. At the same time, it sets the tone for the next section, which deals with 'Abilities and responsibilities'.

In these poems, we are also reminded of the element of personal choice – a reminder that could be said to be thematic throughout the book. In the final analysis, it is up to us to live each moment as we see fit, striving for fullness of awareness and wholeness of being. Such an approach clears the space for living life with an attitude of gratitude. For us, 'a relentless commitment to joy' is the banner we wave before ourselves: An admirable goal when balanced by an attitude of patience and forgiveness when we think we fall short. The alternative is to live in a state of lament.

186

Abilities and responsibilities

We're only human

In this personal writing, the woman is encouraged to recognize life's limitations when it is lived within a physical body. It offers enjoyment as an antidote to burning out under an overload of perceived responsibilities.

We said it once,
we said it twice,
we will say it
a hundred times
that you work and live in
the confinement of your body
and your life.

You are wanted and
needed by so many,
and live your own in the
snippets of time left.

Drop your latent feelings of failure,
give your rebound a chance,
look around as in meditation,
let your mandala of life go from one good
to the other.

Take a deep breath and refocus.
Use each other as balance.
We know you do, and that is okay.
Rebound, rebirth, and restart – and enjoy the moment.

The sky's the limit

This is a personal writing for a woman on her fortieth birthday.

We recognize that the pace of your development increases daily. You know, as we know, that there is no limit to the sky. Limitation is a word without true meaning because there isn't any. It is the person who limits his or her Self.

This writing honours the limitless capacity and potential we all have. In contrast the next one reminds us that there is a limit to how those capacities are put to use.

Enough is enough

This is an anecdotal writing on giving and receiving love, done as a personal consultation for parents of a difficult teenager. This could have gone in the segment on love, but because responsibility seems a central element, we have chosen to place it in this section.

All humanity needs love in great doses. To give it is your responsibility; what they do with it is their responsibility. But yours has finished. To give beyond that is not within your power.

The tone of this writing takes any possessive or ownership quality out of the equation and emphasizes that our personal responsibility is simply to give love. How that love is received is up to the receiver. This kind of interaction is empowering to both giver and recipient, allotting choice and independence to both. It reminded us of the following poem.

Independence meets strength;
Strength meets self-reliance;
And self-reliance breeds confidence;
And confidence breeds happiness;
And happiness fulfils the person.

These are wonderful sentiments which are sometimes hard to live when we feel life's obligations mounting.

The following poem speaks of just how overwhelming the responsibilities of managing our everyday life can feel.

Burdened

Overwhelming minutiae of domestic living.
Endless errands, countless details,
Cluttered moments.
Forgotten contents of a blender,
Whirling round and round.

Here we can tie back into the theme of consolidation as we reflect on its essential tenet: finding peace within oneself, regardless of the conditions. The tedium of life's daily tasks can keep us in a whirl with peacefulness held at bay, or we can regard them as the rent we pay for where and how we live. Is it possible that physical disease takes this to a place of seemingly greater challenge? This question is addressed in the first of the writings to follow.

Attuning the internal and external

In these final writings we begin to look at how we can remain soul directed and still live the human condition. What are the indicators that we are misaligned, and how can we rebalance? In some ways, we could say tracking this has been the prevailing thrust of these last three application chapters.

Dis-ease or actual disease is a powerful indicator that all is not well in the area of letting our soul life infuse our daily activities. Or it can be looked at differently, as was stated in a previous writing. Given that we are in a finite body, disease will be a part of the natural aging process, and it may present an opportunity for us to work with its physical manifestations by using a soul full approach. This shifts soul into a slightly different position. Still a tremendous infuser, it can encourage us to live life fully regardless of the presence of whatever the impediments to health may be, amplifying the interrelationship between body and soul.

The nature of illness –
dealing with external surroundings

Sensitivity to a specific event or substance derives its impact from debility from within the recipient. Illnesses as such are conditions by which the particular nature or body of an individual is unable to cope with challenges and impacts surrounding and interacting with him or her. Succumbing to external stimuli, whatever they may be, is having lost the battle of balance of the self against its surroundings. Do recognize the strength of replenishing and living within non-hostile surroundings as an admission to the fragile balance between man and his environment. Also, do be aware of the great ability of self-regeneration and self-healing if allowed.

The following excerpt from a writing also reinforces the importance of accentuating the positive.

Allow yourself the enjoyment of a positive surrounding.

Encumbrances

In this writing, we are reminded that too tight a schedule leaves little time for personal development. We must turn inward to attain a connection to our chosen purpose on the soul level, and this inward reflection requires time. We also require a certain amount of clarity regarding our needs, be they physical or spiritual.

With a directive from the writings to return to a sense of goal and direction and soulful reflection as a means of problem solving, the following writings provide a perfect answer, offering approaches for goal setting and decision-making, which access our right-brain, intuitive knowings and include the strengthening of the will as well. This is in concert with our overarching goal of integrating soul life into every day.

This is a personal writing for a thirty-five-year-old woman burdened by responsibilities.

To conquer and solve problems, return to sense of goal and direction. The innermost is set to the goal of service. The chance of growth is stunted because of excess input and simple, overbearing fatigue. Force a lifestyle that is more amended to self(ish) needs. Try removal of certain situations by exempting burdens, and leave room for self-development. It is all just temporary. Despite the demands that the nitty-gritty truths of everyday life heap upon us, we must make a consistent commitment to a spiritual discipline if attunement is to be achieved. This is working from the inside out instead of from the outside in, responsive rather than reactive, finding peace within oneself.

Earthbound

This is a personal writing for a man in his thirties who could not overcome his fear of flying.

> *Let go of what holds you.*
> *Adventure is being.*
> *Stoutness of soul is no harm in itself.*
> *Consider enjoyment as passing a test,*
> *And let the body not take itself so seriously.*
> *Rest and let the mind fly.*

LASCAR is the acronym formed by the first letters of each line in this writing. It is an East Indian sailor, an apt metaphor when its message is to take a risk and move out from whatever holds you. It contrasts the first writing in this chapter, 'All is one', where the importance of anchoring the feet is emphasized; the slant of this one is on releasing the body and mind from their tethers. Using the metaphor of flying for release, the term stout reminds us to be dauntless, to advance without fear. At the same time, it encourages the body to not take itself so seriously. Forgetting your vitamins may not mean you must cancel your trip. This gem is a delightful balance of substance and lightness. In its final words, *'rest and let the mind fly'*, it focuses us on two central and recurrent themes of the book: relaxation into what is and expansiveness into the domain of spirit. Or if we dare to use an old cliché, 'Fear of flying inhibits soaring'. Its message is one of encouragement, returning us to a quote from the beginning of the book: 'an upbeat approach to an age-old adat'. Using the same old players – body the vehicle, mind the driver, soul the infuser – our journey in living the human condition is to integrate all three, thus catapulting us into the realm of spirit, 'which soars unfettered by earthly concerns'.

With my questions galore, I reach you

In this final writing, we came humbly back to the team to help us with our conclusion. They reminded us that they, too, are an ever-changing group in a slightly different place: *'We are akin to an earthly group, just in a parallel dimension, revolving like anyone else'*. They asked us to clearly state our intentions – a reminder to direct our question to them in a clear manner. Our intention was a proper wrap up to 'The human condition – windows on the world'. Here is their answer.

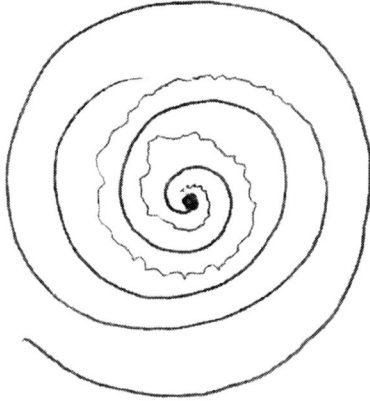

What you think is a problem is what life is all about. How we meet them or rise to the occasion of unfortunate events is what signifies our inner strength. A computer is just a pesky thing; when not obsolete as yet, it functions when taken care of. Life events are a result of choices made, sometimes over prolonged times. Solving them is adapting to avoidance of pain or removing oneself from it totally. Life is not smooth, never was, never is, and never will be. One has to find the courage to move on, keep light in mind, and know that pain hurts.

This writing reminds us that responsibility for our life is our own individual issue. The human condition will include both pleasure and pain. How we deal with it is what counts. The drawing accompanying the writing shows us spiralling inward and encountering life's jagged edges, which eventually smooth out and consolidate with the solid spiral. Then, like the apple in the initial drawing of this chapter, the 'I' can flower, with our uncharted corners charted, so that body, mind, soul, and spirit can live harmoniously as they meet all of life's conditions, 'like holding hands with yourself on a different plane'.

With our eye refocused on the element of personal choice, this poem can help end this chapter. For in the final analysis, it is up to us to live each moment as we see fit. The human condition is indeed human.

Exercise: exploring your humanness – an exercise in detachment

The writings can serve as exercises themselves. Review them and note the one that brings forth an emotional response within you. If more than one arises, choose the one with the most impact. Do a progressive relaxation and, once finished, bring forward the particular situation that the writing triggered. Immerse yourself in the emotion of your situation. Notice your responses and ask why they are there. Now shift back to your more relaxed state, using a circular breath to help if necessary. With full awareness of your situation, imagine that you are floating upward until you reach a vantage point where you can look back at your situation from a place of observation and detachment. From this new perspective, notice your responses to the situation; have they changed? What is the nature of the shift? Now ask yourself what you can do to strengthen and retain this larger perspective. One way to reinforce it is to choose a physical anchor: touch the side of your knee or your ear so that you can use this spot to bring back the qualities that reside in this place of detachment when you find you are getting snagged emotionally. This exercise can be repeated using other situations from the writings or your personal experiences.

Haute Couture

How early do you rise to dress your day?
A closet of colours to choose from.
Drab fields, grey sky, subtle tones,
A canvas of monochrome.
Not for me!
Today I'll splash yellow,
Accent with red fire bush,
Paint the sky a vibrant blue.
White clouds a final ornament.
How early do you rise to dress your day?

Chapter 17
In search of self

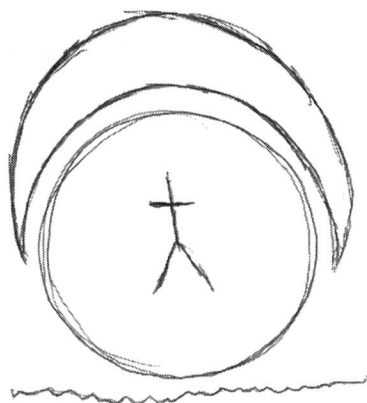

Body is the vehicle,
Mind the driver,
Soul the infuser,
And spirit soars unfettered by earthly concerns.

In these culminating chapters of the book, we reiterate this poem's central teaching. Provided with a myriad of exercises and practices, we have many ways to properly regulate body and mind. Now we can finally move fully into the integration of soul and spirit into our lives. The interplay of all these elements sums up the books intent and takes us back to the introductory chapters. Throughout the overriding question has been, 'How can we function and live to our fullest potential as soulful beings in a human world?'

The following writing, with its reference to the primitive thinking of yesteryear and our emergence into the age of scientific awareness, deepened our understanding of the *how* part of our exploration into navigating these uncharted corners of our consciousness. In the search for the Self, we were required to remember that mind is the driver and the driver is us; now we are being told to take the wheel.

Increased scientific knowledge and expanding technologies have chipped away at the bastions of thousands of years of established belief systems. This presses the individual to search for his place in the increased complexity of the world around him. Nowadays, know-how of the way the world runs is at the tip of our fingers. This is in contrast to the beginning of humankind and long afterwards, where events were often beyond understanding and control. The repetitive return of the yearly sun and moon cycles were observed in order to do the planting. Still, the mechanics of these events were not understood. Not to our credit, the earth remained flat until a few hundred years ago.

Civilizations appeared and disappeared, for although they had great knowledge and understanding, they never matched the knowledge and understanding provided by the scientific escalation of this present time. Many events in daily life in the past were based on superstition and interpretations, which were explainable in a logic that one could understand. Devotions and behaviours were often focused on a higher power, which was believed to govern. Religion and worship were the ways to submit to and appease the unseen forces. Shamans interceded when help was requested and advice wanted. Offerings given to the deities were an important part of their ceremonies, in order to clinch a deal with the almighty powers. Solutions were sought outside of the self, leaving the ancients with a feeling of constant vulnerability.

Presently, some of those former mysteries are resolved. We know that brains work like a computer, many sicknesses are a result of germs or contaminated drinking water, and lightning bolts are a weather phenomenon. Primitive man's thinking had to find a reason outside himself, which then mitigated his existence by appealing to a higher source.

Today, by contrast, the onus is on us, and the tooling is within us. We have been given the knowledge and opportunities to influence the world around us. Thus we are forced to go beyond primary and primitive thinking. What was once called luck and was thought to be someone looking benignly at us, now we know is simply a mathematical roll of the dice. In essence, with all of these changes in our knowledge of our surroundings and the universe, we find we have been placed back into our own hands, relying on our own resources. There are no reasons to look for a designator for our behaviour; we have been handed the reins to our own destiny, and we must live up to our very own expectations. This is not an easy mandate because we are obliged to be in search of the Self in the fullest dimension.

We have been given all of these past writings, which raised the question, 'Who are we? What are we doing with this latitude?' Furthermore, we were told how to better understand ourselves and were directed on how to work with the imparted knowledge.

But who are we? We are individuals composed of the elements of the earth and trace elements of the universe. We all eat, drink, and replenish ourselves from the same sources. Furthermore, we are equipped with the tooling to think, understand, and make moral choices. We live within a personal energy sphere, which intertwines us with our unseen environment, mixing and matching physically with our immediate surroundings. We came onto this earth in consciousness and are gone again, our existence seen over the millennia as an event in time. In essence we are astral beings, and so are our fellow beings, weaponed with all the necessary tooling.

With this directive, we cannot help but search for the Self within the context of an expanded understanding and knowledge of our place within society. This forces us to come to grips with the importance of elasticity in our thinking pattern. Fixed belief systems, which were previously accepted as the norm and established modes of thinking, undermine the flexibility and acceptance of change issues. Frozen in our own thoughts, we inhibit growth of the self and understanding of others. Search for the Self in this expanded way demands that we be actively interested in what is happening in the world and expose ourselves to the variations of life without clouding it with our own thinking platform. For unobstructed thinking, use objectivity, observation, and acceptance. Curiosity and interest, enjoyment and empathy are also viable ways of droning out fixation on one's own intent, allowing us to go beyond subjectivity. When we reach out in such a way, we are truly living on our deeper consciousness level, expanding ourselves into the broader meaning of the universe: pursuing our search of our uncharted corners of consciousness.

The narrative of the development of man emphasizes a change in our movement from primitive, unquestioning beings, willing to submit to the belief in forces outside of our control, to modern mystics informed by science and governed by our own knowings.

In the search for 'Who am I?' and 'What do I represent?', it will serve our development if we clear our field of irrational thought, cut through the wrappings of preconceived notions, and free ourselves of rehashed opinions. We must dare to turn away from the trodden path in order to come up with a fresh view, fitting of change situations. The term 'free thinker' gets new meaning.

In previous writings, we had the opportunity to get an insight into the palette of events and stories as seen by different people, which inhibited their movement towards freedom of thought. Each person is unique, with situations interpreted and expressed in compliance with their own views. Issues are evaluated based on their own remembrances. It is these thoughts and issues that hold us back. Further, our thoughts often create inaccurate pictures and disturbing thought forms, like the proverbial elephant described by various people, each one able to feel only a particular part: tail, trunk, toenail, or head, which when reported became a form unrecognizable by anyone. In our team's words,

One person's sunny day is another's burning of the crops.

Throughout these writings, the messages continue to point out that we are responsible for our own self-development. Seeking and questing for answers to the why of existence, we must look within and incorporate our uncharted corners of consciousness into our daily life. We will then be in tune with the whisperings from our soul.

The sacredness knows
That one is unique,
Worthy of caring
About Self and where one lives.
Walk lightly,
Walk lovingly,
Walk attentively.

Chapter 18
The end, the beginning

Our uncharted corners – a never-ending exploration

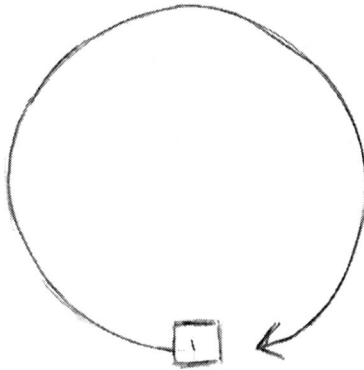

Having absorbed the material and encouragement from our spiritual teaching team over the years, we offer our own conclusions and observations. The richness of all the writings put us on the path of self-search and understanding. Often the nitty-gritty details of self-evident issues masked the fact that we are unique integrated unities. The simple ABCs of these details were only the markers of a much deeper thought. An alphabet used in exquisite sentences can become the world's bestseller – but it also could become gibberish personified. Our dialogue and writing observed the monumental wisdom that permeates the deeper thinking. It was this energy source, which we all represent in our forms, with which we corresponded and communicated. Bringing this book to conclusion is an awesome if not impossible task. The teachings go on and on – always there for the asking. For this, we thank our team.

Having begun our studies in the 1980s and completing our writing in 2012, we could say that time has indeed been our friend. At the start we felt tentative, and shared these feelings with you. Early on we questioned the veracity of what we were doing, but over time these feelings dissipated. We grew into the understanding that this source of wisdom which we had accessed was not limited to us alone, but rather was a universal source into which we could all tap. As so aptly put by Gerbrig, 'All we did was go to the big lending library' – and we want you to know that we are all card carriers.

Yes, we scrutinized, studied, tested, debated, practiced, studied, and practiced some more – no wonder this took forty years. But now we present this book to you with full confidence that in the process of writing, we have exercised our full potential, have been all we could. We know that each and every one of you has the ability to do the same. We hope this book will help guide you in your process.

As we conclude, we do so with the knowledge that, as we end we also begin, with the impetus for continued exploration and growth. Like the snake biting its tail, depicted in the drawing, we are back to square one. We sign off with confidence that the information contained in this manuscript provides you with a rich basis for self-search and self-resourcing into your personal uncharted corners. Our mandate is complete.

Logic on the eternal level is without words.

References

Aberdeen, P., Naisbett, J. (1986). *Reinventing the corporation.* New York: Little, Brown.

Bach, R. (2006). *The bridge across forever: A true love story* (Paperback). New York: Harper Paperbacks.

Benson, H., & Klipper, M. Z. (2000). *The relaxation response.* Toronto: HarperCollins Canada.

Benson, H. (1985). *Beyond the relaxation response.* New York: Berkley Books.

Brugh, J. (1979). *Joy's way: A map for the transformational journer.* Los Angeles: Tarcher.

Chopra, D. (1990). *Quantum healing: Exploring the frontiers of mind/ body medicine.* New York: Bantam Books.

Chopra, D. (1994). *Seven spiritual laws of success.* Novato, CA: New World Library.

Chopra, D. (2001). *Perfect health – Revised and updated: The complete mind body guide* (Rev. ed.). New York: The Crown Publishing Group.

Chopra, D. (2003). *The Chopra Centre cookbook: Nourishing body and soul.* Hoboken, NJ: John Wiley & Sons.

Cousins, N. (2005). *Anatomy of an illness as perceived by the patient.* New York: Norton.

Donne, J. (2008). *No man is an island* (G. Martin, HTML format). Retrieved February 25, 2010, form http://www.phrases.org.uk/meanings/no-man-is-an-island.html (Original work published 1624).

Gardner, K. (1994). *A rainbow path* [CD]. USA: Ladyslipper (Originally published 1984).

Gerber, G. (2002). *Exploring vibrational medicine* [Audio tape]. Louisville, CO: Sounds True.

Hazlitt, W. (2007). *On living to one's self* (P. Madden, HTML format). Retrieved February 24, 2010, from http://essays.quotidiana.org/hazlitt/living_to_ones_self/ (Original work published 1821).

Juhan, D., Dychtwald, K. (2002). *Job's body: A handbook for bodywork.* Barrytown, NY: Station Hill Press.

Lennon, J., McCartney, P. (1965). "All you need is love" [Audio recording]. New York: EMI Blackwood Music Inc.

Lennon, J., Ono, Y. (1980). "Beautiful boy (Darling boy)" [Audio recording]. Los Angeles: Geffen Records.

Lingerman, H. (1983). *The healing energies of music.* Wheaton, IL: Quest Books/Theosophical Publishing House.

Liskin, J., (1966). The life and work of Milton Trager, MD. Barrytown, NY: Station Hill Press.

Liston, J. (1996). *Moving medicine: The life and work of Milton Trager, MD.* Barrytown, NY: Station Hill Press.

Mairi, A., (2006). Trager for self-healing: a practical guide for living in the present moment. H. J. Kramer Books, in joint venture with New World Library.

McLuhan. M. (2001). *The medium is the message* (New ed.). Berkeley, CA: Gingko Press.

Montgomery, R. (1984). *Strangers among us.* Greenwich, CT: Fawcett Press.

Moore, T. (1994). *Soul mates.* New York: Harper Perennial.

Osborne, M., Stevenson, J. (Directors). (2008). *Kung Fu Panda* (Movie). USA: DreamWorks Animation.

Random House. (2005). *Random House dictionary* (Rev. ed.). New York: Random House.

Rubin, W. S. (1985). *Dada and the surrealist art.* New York: Abrams.

Seagal, S., Horne, D. (2002, September). *The human dynamics body of knowledge and its implications for education: A brief account.* Retrieved February 1, 2010, from http://www.newhorizons.org/strategies/styles/horne.htm

Seagal, S. Horne. D. (1997) *Human dynamics: A new framework for understanding people and realizing the potential in our organizations.* Pegasus Communications, (Revised version on the way).

Selye, H. H. B. (1978). *The stress of life* (2nd ed.). New York: McGraw-Hill.

Simonton, C., Matthews-Simonton, S. (1986). *Getting well again: A step-by-step, self-help guide to overcoming cancer for patients and their families.* New York: Bantam Books.

Stern, J. (1989). *Edgar Cayce: The sleeping prophet* (New ed.). New York: Bantam Books.

Trager, M., Guadagno, C. (1988). *Trager mentastics: movement as a way to agelessness.* Barrytown, NY: Station Hill Press.

About the authors

Gerbrig Berman
The beginning? Who knew?

It was a day like most of our days on a surgical floor of a hospital outside Jerusalem. I had been working there for a few years as a nurse and felt fortunate to be part of the dedicated medical staff. Ours was a cancer ward, and because of the specific nature of the disease and the many repeat admissions, we got to know most of the patients very well. We shared many of their victories and also their sadnesses. We tried as much as possible to be there for all. We had all chosen to work in this particular area of nursing, and though not always easy, we found it most fulfilling.

One particular day sticks in my mind. Looking back I realize it began a process, one that changed the way I thought. But I'm getting ahead of myself.

So that day was like any other day. But with the addition of a shortage of staff and some very ill people – a day like any other – but in this case, even more challenging. One elderly lady was not feeling well after her mastectomy. The fact that we were very busy and barely had enough time to answer her frequent calls did not make the situation any better. She was crying out and ringing her bell constantly. We could hear her throughout the halls. The sound was disconcerting – not only for us but for the other patients. It started to wear us down.

Finally I went to my office. I shut the door, sat down, closed my eyes, and took a deep breath, not knowing where to go or what to do. My mind was on overload, and I knew I had to smooth out my thoughts. I happened to have a pencil in my hand and paper on my desk, and I started to doodle. When I glanced down I noticed I had drawn a stick figure of a woman with one breast missing. I felt embarrassed. What had I done? Had I invaded someone's privacy? I tried to scratch the drawing out. Then I noticed that those scratched out lines depicted two arms encircling the stick person. I was dumbfounded! Then, since I had nothing to lose, I decided to follow what the picture had shown me to do. I got up, walked to the poor lady, and put my arms around her. I asked her to tell me exactly what she wanted us to know and what she thought we could do to help her. She eased a little more into my arms, started to cry, and thanked me for being there. First she apologized for having been so demanding and then she sobbed and started to tell me her story. Her misery came pouring out: she had lost her family in the Holocaust, her friends were old, and nobody had been in to visit her. She felt so alone. When she finished her story, she smiled and told me all she had wanted was a hug and to not have to feel alone. Having listened, I promised her I would be the one changing her dressings from that moment on. I gave her a specific time and assured her it would allow us to spend some time together. From that moment on she was able to express herself, share her memories, and let us know when she needed something. Her relationships with other patients and staff changed drastically for the better, and after some prodding she phoned her friends to tell them how she was coming along.

If anyone was surprised and questioned what had just happened, it was me. What did this all mean? I was young, well travelled, had worked hard, and had many friends. My life was interesting and tumultuous. Born in Indonesia, and having spent my childhood in a Japanese prisoner of war camp, I relished how good my present life was. I was 'standing with both feet in the world', but that day I found out that all of that was not enough. I realized that for some reason I had stepped into another mode of functioning, one that was not part of my everyday venues. I felt as though an inner door had opened in me, one that offered me a different view of myself in relation to myself and

others. I obviously had stepped into a behaviour previously untapped. This incident had started my road to change. It was the beginning of accepting that there was a place for operating on different levels of awareness and that my drawings could be utilized in a very practical manner. Through unlocking myself, a door had opened for another person. After that, it was clear to me what direction to go.

I was intrigued. I began looking for answers. As I reviewed what had happened I realized a series of circumstances had brought me to this point. It had been a day like many others, and like my colleagues I was only doing my job. The critical element seemed to be that things were not working out. Moments like these, when our old ways don't provide the answers we need, force us to look at other options. For me it was the doodling. And as I thought more about it, it occurred to me that I had been doodling for years. What I hadn't realized before was that those doodles were representations of my thoughts, and as I continued to draw, those thoughts formed words. I paid attention to these thoughts and wrote them down in order not to lose them. Didn't Mozart hear the music in his mind and write it down? Don't poets hear or feel the words they think and then write them down? Doesn't everyone at some time think, *Should I or shouldn't I?* before a decision is made? It all made ultimate sense to me.

Still, it took many years before I started come to terms with all of this, before I allowed myself to see my multidimensional form. As a young adult I had been busy getting in touch with the world around me. My exploration did not include something that others might find 'spooky'. But slowly, when I was in doubt about events around me, I began to take my 'time out' more and more. Maybe I was not so different from people who pray or meditate. But still, I tried to find the words to explain, in a logical way, what I was experiencing. I knew and know that it bothers people when concepts are not explainable and cannot be replicated as science would like.

Finally, however, curiosity did get the upper hand. I went back to school to study psychology, realizing that the mind is a marvellous thing. I also thought that what I needed was the proper vocabulary and wondered if there would have been studies done in this area. I actually was horrified that people would think about me as being different and dabbling in odd behaviour. I preferred to keep quiet about it. This seemed the easiest thing to do.

Then I met Shelly, who happened to see one of my doodles and asked about it. She has qualities that were not my strength. Shelly immediately began pointing out the application of the messages and directives given in these drawings and writings.

We seemed to complement each other in many ways. So we started our studies. We committed ourselves to a weekly study sessions focus on the wisdom of the writings. We focused on how we could access, understand and work with this multidimensional self. In the beginning we did not know that we were being sent to spiritual kindergarten.

The drawings and writings began by giving us basic lessons. Later on we noticed that there was a sequence to these lessons. As we often said before, we were intrigued.

We do not think we are in any way unusual women. We are women who happened to be curious about our larger purpose in life and our uncharted corners. And so, we have spent many years working at understanding and dealing with issues in a more in-depth manner. We are not different from anyone who makes a moral decision based on an inner dialogue or has compassion for the world and society in which we live. We simply made a conscious decision to step outside of the personal ego-driven self into our larger Self. We just happened to have written our findings down and have translated these teachings into a practical format that we were able to use in our respective careers.

Today we continue to hold on to the awareness of the richness of our human Spiritual Nature. We realize that our Spiritual aspect, referred to in the book as Our Deeper Self, hopefully broadens our abilities and understanding of the world around us.

Shelly Siskind

How often do we choose to walk on a path well known to us, one that we've trod with comfort many times before? This would be a good descriptor of my choice at twenty-one years of age. I was a bride of four years who had moved from Toronto to London, Ontario, leaving my fledgling medical social work and possible career as a social worker behind. I would live with my newly inducted lawyer husband, establish a home, and begin a family.

It was the mid-sixties, and I had settled comfortably into being a stay-at-home wife and mom. Fortunately, there were just enough projects outside the house to satisfy my Aquarian callings to change the world. My time was filled raising children, entertaining, establishing the Block Parent Safety Program, volunteering at the art gallery, and selling art. You could say with some accuracy that I was a conveniently conventional woman.

Who could have predicted that the call I answered two short years later from a woman named Gerbrig was the 'swish' of the karmic tail that led both our lives in a very different direction. When she and her husband moved to London, a Toronto friend had suggested they look us up. Neither Gerbrig nor I suspected that from the moment we connected, her life and mine would be intimately intertwined.

Perhaps the extraordinary always does spring from the ordinary, and the beginnings of our friendship were predictably mundane. But our paths began crossing more and more, either socially or through the various community projects with which we were involved. As young mothers with growing families there was little room in our lives for much more, or so we thought. But perhaps there is indeed a larger plan and dimensions other than the one right under our feet. And perhaps for movement into waters less charted to happen, a somewhat different foundation must be laid, and certainly we must be pushed out of our comfort zone.

In retrospect, I realize that my husband has most often been the impetus for my moving into those uncomfortable places. In this instance it was his bad back that compelled me to take a lay massage course. It was this course that led me into an area previously unknown to me. My interest was tweaked as I was introduced to a variety of holistic therapies. I learned how these approaches complemented the standard medical treatments and often brought healing to conditions not touched

by a straight medical approach. These realizations set me on a course of extensive training in a variety of holistic disciplines. I continued in serious studies for the next ten years, beginning an exploration into a variety of fields: energy work, Trager bodywork, body scanning, and

other related mind-body fields. Both Gerbrig and I had branched tentatively and quietly out into these holistic and expansive health-related areas. I became certified as a Trager practitioner and tutor, while Gerbrig, who had already been nursing in many countries, enriched her background with studies in psychology and palliative care.

Our weekly study sessions continued throughout all of our working and training lives. As kindred spirits adrift in new waters living in a conservative city, it was a natural for Gerbrig and me to gravitate towards one another. We were able to discuss and explore more spiritually focused topics in comfort and safety. We started to study

Gerbrig's intuitive drawings. I was awed by their accuracy, and having done body scans that produced Pillsbury Doughboy drawings and information, I needed no convincing that the teachings, accessed from our multidimensional self, were useful.

Eventually, Gerbrig and I shared office space, from which I did my Trager body work and she

taught meditation and did supportive consultations. Later I opened a stress management business and rented a building, which housed many holistic practitioners. In addition to my Trager practice I branched out into teaching and speaking on stress management and self-care, developing programs for businesses, social service agencies, and in a series of colleges and universities. Recently I

designed courses for Trager practitioners and students that are taught internationally.

But I am getting ahead of myself.

Over time I had realized that harnessing our intuitive and body skills had value. But with a strong interest in reaching a larger number of people I had needed to find a language that could take all of this information out of the realm of 'woo woo' and make it sound sensible and concrete. I was constantly seeking new descriptors. Although I relentlessly searched for accreditation and degrees, what I wanted to study was not offered at the colleges or universities. My training was and still is always on my feet and in the field. And the information flow comes to me from the place of silent inquiry and emptiness to which we allude throughout the book. In progressive years I realized that what I was working with all along was 'the Self as a resource'.

Worthy of mention is that the work of Dr Milton Trager, and Human Dynamics, the work of Dr Sandra Seagal, greatly influenced my life. Today Dr. Trager, a medical doctor, is regarded as a pioneer in the mind-body field. He perfectly described how the endorphins and other amino acids work. But sixty years ago, science had not yet provided the vocabulary to explain what Milton knew to be, so and the statement, 'My practitioners develop a state of relaxation in themselves, and their clients catch it like the measles' in those days sounded quite outlandish! In addition to training in bodywork skills, my deeper understanding of humankind was honed by Human Dynamics, the work and training of Dr Sandra Seagal. Sandra, a trained psychologist and Jungian analyst, following an intuitive experience conducted in-depth research and solidified her understandings into a profound system that explains how people integrate and express themselves in the world around them. The personal development side of Sandra's work advanced both Gerbrig's and my meditative and discernment skills in the area of human functioning.

Trager and Human Dynamics are described in detail in chapter four, 'The whole in one: perfecting techniques in soul development'.

The work on this book has been an endeavour of ours for many years. The writings have been a backstay not only to our work but to ourselves. For me, these writings were a door opener to the creative miracle available. I understand that our spiritual self is the dynamo behind our physical presence, and I feel that it is easy to dismiss this realization as we go about our activities in our busy world.

Gerbrig and I knew that these understandings were not to be held, and so after much prodding, we send these insights of our uncharted corners into the world.

Glossary

allopathic: the practice of conventional medicine.

altered consciousness: any state of mind which is outside our everyday conscious functions.

astral beings: humans in their non-physical energy form a form, which accompanies them through life and survives them in death.

astral body/astral field: the energetic or electromagnetic field that surrounds our body; it accompanies a person through life and survives one in death.

astral level: a plane of conscious outside the physical; the space we go to in between lives.

attunement: to bring into harmony; at-one-ment.

altruism: unselfish concern for the welfare of others.

body: the vehicle, the physical container.

Buddhism: a religion originated by Buddha, holding that suffering is caused by desire and that the way to end this suffering is through enlightenment *(Random House Dictionary)*.

caul: a membrane that sometimes covers the head of a foetus, seen by some as a sign of second sight.

chakra: the body's energy centres aligned along the spine, from the base of the spine to a place above the skull.

channelled material: written or spoken material received from the non-physical realm, which is presented without scrutiny; the receiver of the information is merely a receptacle, the physical form through which the information can pass.

clair audial: the messages are heard.

clair sensual: the messages are felt.

clair visual: the messages are seen.

direct dialling: clarifying what it is you want to know from the dimensions of the soul and then making contact through your deeper self.

enlightenment: a state of wholeness and oneness with all that is, devoid of longing for all things associated with the physical plane; sometimes said to be the place of unconditional love.

expanded consciousness: the ability of our mind to go into the conscious part and into the unconscious.

hedonism: devotion to pleasure as a way of life.

hi-fi: a focused state of personal alertness which logs us on to our deeper dimensions. In our text it refers to our well-honed ability to receive information from the meditative realms where there are no words, and as we bring it through our personal filter, we do so with as little distortion as possible.

higher Self: or soul self is sometimes referred to as the transpersonal self, the aspect of us that is freed from the constraints of the ego and feels a connection to all that is.

integral: essential to the completeness of the whole.

integral Self, integral intrinsic being: our superconscious which surpasses both conscious memory and unconscious forgotten memory. Body + mind + soul = the integral Self.

integrated Self: the integrated person not only accepts his or her physical world but also tries to understand the growth of his spiritual part and his love for creation.

intrinsic: belonging to a thing by its very nature.

intrinsic Self: our right brain, our feeler aspects.

integrative Self: the aspect or our being which seeks wholeness through balance of body, mind, and soul. The integrative self is sometimes called the third eye.

karma: a philosophy in Hinduism and Buddhism; actions seen as bringing upon oneself inevitable results, good or bad either in this life or in a reincarnation *(Random House Dictionary)*. Karma is the working out of whatever learning the soul has not yet accomplished in its path towards creativity and love.

kundalini: Sanskrit for 'snake' or 'serpent power', so-called because it is believed to lie like a serpent in the root chakra at the base of the spine. It is described as an unconscious, instinctive, or libidinal force (Wikipedia).

left brain: the portion of the brain that houses linear deductive thinking.

multidimensional self: same as the integral self; it is the self in all aspects, body, mind, and soul.

mandala, mantra, mudra: three traditional Buddhist methods of self-sourcing; all three are tools for focusing and centring in the now.

mandala: a visual, an expression, or a form, again coming from Sanskrit, which literally means centre or circle. Its traditional design often utilizes the circle, the symbol of the cosmos in its entirety, and the square symbol of the earth or the man-made world. Broken down, 'mano' means 'mind' and 'dala' means 'expansion and unfoldment'. 'Dala' also means 'a device or tool that evokes an expansion of consciousness'. In our writings the term 'mandala' refers to drawings executed while in a meditative, right-brain state and that begin within the confines of a circle. Through the use of a mandala, the mind can increase its content or range. (This definition is taken from two sources: *Mandala* by Jose Arguelles and *Unfolding Through Art* by Namgyal Rinpoche.)

mantra: a sound, a combination of sacred symbols which forms a nucleus of spiritual energy. This serves as a magnet to attract or a lens to focus spiritual vibrations. The root 'mano' in Sanskrit means 'to think'; 'tra' comes from 'trai', meaning 'to protect from the bondage of the phenomenal world'. Therefore, mantra means 'the thought that liberates and protects'. Its power is felt to increase through the repetition of sounds, such as 'aum'.

mudra: a position. Mudra is a gesture or posture like tai chi, a concentration on movement which becomes a ritual.

meditation: to clear the mind of distracting thoughts, in order to think in a contemplative way.

mens sana in corpore sano: Latin for 'a sound mind in a sound body'.

mind: the driver; it is deliberate, calculative, and issue oriented. It is a vibrational lever that facilitates change when lessons are learned.

moksha: a Hindu term for enlightenment.

meridians: the lines through which energy is transmitted throughout the body.

negative: as used in this book, it refers to anything the person deems non-nurturing, supportive, and replenishing. The impact of these elements may allude to our various aspects: our physical body, our emotional state, or our spiritual condition.

non-physical body: also referred to as the vibrational lever, it is sometimes known as the subtle or energetic body. Both mind and the non-physical body are referred to as vibrational levers, however they operate from different fields: the mind utilizes conscious thought, and the non-physical body shifts the energy itself.

non-physical level: can also be referred to as the astral or etheric plane.

positive: as used in this book, it refers to anything the person deems nurturing, supportive, and replenishing. The impact of these elements may allude to our various aspects: our physical body, our emotional state, or our spiritual condition.

psychosomatic: 'psyche' means of the mind and 'soma' means of the body; the psychosomatic is the connection of mind and body.

psychosomatic approach: a healing technique which acknowledges that our thoughts have the ability to impact the body's well-being either positively or negatively. A term which sometimes had a negative connotation, implying that one's dis-eases or diseases were a product of the imagination.

prana: our vital principle or life force.

psychic blueprint: the enduring map that accompanies us from many lifetimes. It can be likened to our DNA. One charts our physical realm, one our psychic. This blueprint is sometimes referred to as our psychic code or psychic make-up.

psychic: that which pertains to the human soul or mind.

reincarnation: rebirth of the soul in a new body (*Random House Dictionary*).

right brain: the portion of the brain which houses abstract sensing and feeling.

self: an aspect of soul still influenced by what surrounds its physical form. In small caps "self" refers to the personality or ego. When capitalized it is synonymous with the higher or transpersonal Self.

Self-awareness: an understanding of oneself in all aspects of being, body, mind, and soul.

self-sourcing: the search for self-awareness.

silent self: the wordless place to which we retreat within ourselves.

soul: the infuser of essential higher thought. With its reminiscing and transitory nature, it is the memory bank of all our former lives. Soul is the aspect of our essence, which remains unaffected by outer influences. The path of the soul stays the same throughout our many existences; what is affected is the form through which it will express in our present life.

soul destination: the search for wholeness in body, mind, and spirit.

soul group: a collection of disembodied souls who reside in the non-earthly dimension and with whom one feels a spiritual connection.

soul purpose: the goals a soul chooses to achieve in all its lifetimes; its raison d'etre for reincarnating into earthly existences.

spirit: the guiding principle of conscious life; it animates the body and mediates between body and soul. It is the aspect of us that soars, unfettered by earthly concerns – hence the term 'free spirit'.

spiritual discipline: commitment to a consistent practice whose focus is spiritual alignment and integration (e.g., yoga, tai chi, meditation).

superconscious: also referred to as our integral intrinsic being; the part of our consciousness which surpasses both conscious memory and unconscious forgotten memory; a place far beyond the realm of self where all is one.

tabula rasa: from the Latin words 'tabula', which means 'slate', and 'rasa', which means 'erased', it refers to the mind as a clean slate. In the development of a person, it is the child in its uncluttered state, prior to socialization or indoctrination.

thought manifest: the soul as it chooses to express itself into physical form through thought.

transitory vehicle: an alternate term used to describe the body.

vibrations: wavelike emanations of energy to which interpretation gives positive and negative connotations.

visualization: forming a mental image.

wholistic: therapies that seek to unearth the root causes of disease. They search for answers within the interrelationships of body, mind, and soul.

Whisperings from the soul

A collection of musings and mini meditations

Introduction

These small meditations are a compilation of the wisdom and inspirational sayings contained in our primary work *Uncharted Corners of Consciousness*. It is our hope that this whimsical digest form will invite you to retreat into a contemplative place which is purely your own. These musings are punctuated with spiritual energy points, which can add sparkle to your experience.

Body, Mind, Soul, and Spirit

Body is the vehicle,
Mind the driver,
Soul the infuser.

Body is the what,
Mind the how,
And soul the why.

To live with one's body, mind, spirit, and soul linked is like holding hands with yourself on a different plane.

Nourishing the body, nourishing the mind, and treasuring the self on the soul level frees us from any action which favours functioning in a one-sided mode.

Body and Mind

A crystal is a form which nature has allowed.
Our body is a form which nurture has allowed.

Body has a present presence, a focus in our total function as a part-time transportation.

The degree of stress one experiences is often determined by the response one has towards what is outside oneself and how the mind interprets these events.

We live within and through our mindset, creating our own scenarios.

Our emotions and demeanour register themselves in a concrete manner. They express on our face or in our stance as joy or sorrow.

Mind, the fooler, can be trapped in its own lies.

Mind is a critical, self-governing focus of the self.

Frozen in our own thoughts, we inhibit growth of the self and understanding of others.

We live within and through our mindset, creating our own scenario. We are in essence our own masters.

Thought is the reason behind any result.

Logic is very superficial; it serves everyday lingo to sort things out. Logic on the eternal level is without words.

The body senses,
The mind thinks,
And the soul brings peace.

Soul

Soul is the part of us that first houses the sparkling realization that there is more to us than our mere physical container.

The soul is the reminiscing and transitory vehicle, our essence which is unaffected by outer influences and is able to glimpse a larger picture – past, present, and future.

In our personal continuum,
everything is just an event.
Only soul is immortal.

Soul is universally based, with a depth of caring, understanding, and love that does not turn its back on the human but sees it as a small part of the total.

Soul the infuser is an unconditional space within the self which feels one with all, where blaming and resentment are unknown and material issues find no place.

Soul is the infuser of essential higher thought. Its thought process descends to where deeper love and caring dwell, to the place of feeling, the source of commitment and responsibility.

In the soul dimension, birth is a way of grounding a soul to a space in which it can find relevance.

Soul can be seen as an apparatus of function, the nerve cell tuned to its high aspirations, a translator of a far-away impulse.

In the search of self, there comes a time when the need to meet the soul on its own turf becomes a haunting wish.

Contact on the soul level is a transcendental experience when time stands still, future and past are one, and commitments drop.

In the realm of soul expression, the goal is learning and growth.

On the soul level, man knows all; on the earth level, the choice might be simplicity.

Every soul expression is founded within the core of its experiences: its failures, its victories, its retributions of past events.

Soul groups are partnerships – nothing extraordinary, just the power of the ordinary which, when accessed, is a channel more boundless than the Internet.

Soul groups: 'We are here, you are there' is but a concept; so is space, so is time, so is essence.

Soul mates, often so highly exalted, can also be the ones driving negative impact within our lifetime.

The soul is eternal; it will never be young or old.

Spirit

Spirit is the aspect of us that soars, unfettered by earthly concerns.

Spirit is a guiding principle of conscious life, animating body and mediating between body and soul.

Remove any misconceptions that the element called spirit lives in a domain separate from that which we call the material.

Conscious Living

Live your deeper meaning.
Keep clarity in your eye,
Breathe the richness of what is around,
Savour the flavour so to say.
Bring the laughter back.

Let it be known that life is less of a mystery than what we think!

Give energy a boost and uplift confidence.

Goals are misleading words for work to be done.
With work to be done, set out to the doing.

Keep your feet on the ground, strive for a healthy mind in a healthy body, and all will unfold as it should.

Hardship is as deep as needed and as hard as allowed.

What you think is a problem is what life is all about.

How we meet our problems or rise to the occasion of unfortunate events is what signifies our inner strength.

One person's sunny day is another's burning of the crops.

Put sorrow where it belongs, but also put happiness in its place.

To be self-governed is to be liberated; harmful aspects are mind made.

In order to express fully oneself in the world as a caring, charitable, non-judgemental entity, we demand the dexterity spirit brings.

An attitude of simplicity will protect against overindulgence.

We do without doing,
Know without knowing,
Find without seeking.

Each turn of events is left to destiny, and reflection upon it is what makes us whole.

Nature invites us to discover her many offerings, to attune to her moods and rhythms, and to notice all that surrounds us.

Let time and demands of a physical surround be a pleasant brook on which the mind sails and enjoys the landscape going by.

Limitation is a word without true meaning because there isn't any. It is the person who limits himself or herself.

Seeing ourselves as part of creative spirit and a member of a larger soul essence makes us, in this existence, more compassionate and understanding humans.

Beauty does not run away.

Let the positive not become your negative.

Dealing with oneself in a proper way encourages others to do likewise.

Treasuring Life

Live to the fullest. Only then do you live the best life possible.

Take each day as a wonder, and life as a bouquet of multi-variety, so to say.

A lifetime is a commodity too precious to waste by looking constantly over one's shoulder.

Just living is not using your potentiality.

Operating on a footing of deliberateness can only serve to support the fluidity of self and enhance our joy in living life to the fullest.

Life is living, not a race towards achievement.

Too much introspective worry is living through an artificial screen.

There is nothing wrong with thinking about death.
It shows a capacity to think beyond one's boundaries.

Wishing death is leaving out the main course and snacking one's health away.

Suicide is merely a postponement of challenges to be conquered.

Rise above the din of living without being afraid to be part of it.

In the dynamics of life, we are like stones in a bag polishing each other.

Our life is the harvest of the seeds we sow.

Learning

Learning is like the flow of a stream; it soothes the thought and moves to unknown destinies.
Independence meets strength,
Strength meets reliance,
Self-reliance breeds confidence.
Confidence breeds happiness,
And happiness fulfils the person.

Forever going with a goal in mind is the essence of our spiritual bind.

Bad karma is whatever you are not. Good karma is using what you got.

There is no karmic letdown if you are not perfect. Working hard is already ribbon burning.

Life's dilemmas, which we repeatedly find ourselves in, seem so often to take on a similar form.

Avoid judgement; discernment will be enough to guide your steps.

To judge either self or others diminishes; to accept expands.

To connect with the deeper Self requires a retreat from the known self.

It is said that the vessel has to be emptied before it can be filled again.

Meditation

Meditation is what raises the thought to a mindless level of quiet.

Watch the pebble
Listen to the sea.

Mandala: the path a thought walks on.

Mandalas are doodles of the mind.

Meditation is the retreat from calculation and the emptying of the self.

What is important on the earth level does not even exist on the contemplative one.

Dream work is a treasure trove, a gold mine, a dialogue on the sly.

Dreams are notes from the unconscious, unopened letters to yourself.

Time

There is no hurry; we have eternity to work within.

If life consists of only one edition, we should have been able to cancel our subscription.

It serves us well to remember that regression is reality on a different level.

We cannot judge the next step until we have taken this one, and we sure can't judge tomorrow's walk!

Life is just a fraction of eternity, a series of breaths with a beginning and an end.

Change & Growth

Self-growth takes us to a realm of its own, a flight in space with an enjoyment of freedom.

If the soul were to choose a lifetime of searching for inner perfection, we might find a clue within the repetitive stumbling blocks we encounter.

Simplicity is in perfection.
What perfection is in simplicity!
One does not exist without the other.

Drop one, gain one.
Gain one, drop one.

Drop a physical need,
Gain a spiritual need,
Drop one and gain one.

Positive increases positivity and snowballs to infinite possibilities – as does the negative.

Enjoyment of functioning within a world which feels compatible makes us feel compatible, and we act accordingly.

Be a pulsating, aware person, vibrating and activating each last cell and molecule inside you.

Major decisions and changes are less of an external motive than a result of inside growth.

We function to answer our destiny, regardless of our circumstances.

Physical change is a demand of maturing.
Spiritual change is a demand of being.

Obligation is self-imposed; there is no must.

Lots of suffering is caused by home-concocted worries.

Love

Life is important when love touches it.

The realities of life make their demands.
The realities of love make known their wants.

The care of the living, the love which transcends, meets no boundaries at the end.

What we love and feel in our self is what our whole essence is about.

Understanding the parameters of love is knowing when bondage ends and duty takes over.

Until I perceive, I cannot see.
Until I see, I cannot love as I would.

Creating

We are the generators within our own creation.

Thought has the potential to create in physical form. Mind is, in effect, your creator.

Self-pride and self-confidence enable us to trust in our own ability, to manage and perform well in the world.

Through saying 'thanks' and 'please', we bring a deeper dimension into our everyday life, moving the mystical into the mundane.

We all will eventually create a unique picture which expresses the choices we have made.

Our interest is what keeps our thought forms alive.

Liberated from material and physical constraints, we are free to roam in the realm of inspiration – random acts of creativity!

Drawings can be visual reminders of an abstract thought which might otherwise have left our consciousness.

We test the borders of our creative potential through curiosity, focus on experimentation with our creative part, spiritual mobility, activity, and questioning.

Creative thought is often drowned out through repetition on the beaten path.

CPSIA information can be obtained at www.ICGtesting.com
Printed in the USA
LVOW062036230712

291220LV00007B/10/P